The
Tricky
Trivia
Challenge

Also available in Beaver by Susan Abbott

Join the Record Breakers
The Smelly Socks Joke Book
How To Become Famous

The Tricky Trivia Challenge

Susan Abbott

Illustrated by Jan Smith

Beaver Books

A Beaver Book
Published by Arrow Books Limited
62–5 Chandos Place, London WC2N 4NW

An imprint of Century Hutchinson Ltd

London Melbourne Sydney Auckland
Johannesburg and agencies throughout the world

First published 1988
Text © Victorama Ltd 1988
Illustrations © Century Hutchinson Ltd 1988

This book is sold subject to the condition that
it shall not, by way of trade or otherwise, be lent,
resold, hired out, or otherwise circulated without the
publisher's prior consent in any form of binding or
cover other than that in which it is published and
without a similar condition including this condition
being imposed on the subsequent purchaser.

Set in Century Schoolbook
by JH Graphics Ltd, Reading

Made and printed in Great Britain
by Anchor Brendon Ltd
Tiptree, Essex

ISBN 0 09 956370 3

Contents

Introduction

The Tricky Trivia Challenge Quiz is designed to test your general knowledge – and your specific knowledge – of a wide variety of subjects. There is a total of 132 quizzes in the book and, generally speaking, those at the beginning are the easiest and those at the end are the most difficult.

Each quiz consists of ten questions, each of which deals with the same subject category throughout the book. For example, all questions 1 deal with TV and movies. The categories are as follows:

1. TV and movies
2. True or false – statements to which this question must be answered.
3. Sport
4. Science
5. Geography
6. Pop music – current hits, 'classics' and some traditional songs
7. The natural world – plants, animals and natural phenomena
8. The arts – music (apart from pop), theatre, opera, ballet, literature
9. Famous people, both historical and living
10. Anything goes – general knowledge with questions on a wide variety of topics

Each category gives as wide a coverage as possible.

There are a number of ways of enjoying the book. The simplest is to dip in here and there and see how many questions you can answer. But if you want to be more competitive, try the Tricky Trivia Challenges.

The Trivia Mastermind Challenge

You can use this simply as a test for yourself, or as a contest with other players. The idea is to work your way through the book from Quiz 1 to Quiz 132 attempting all the questions in each quiz in numerical order. Award yourself one point for each question answered correctly in Quizzes 1 to 20, two points for each question answered correctly in Quizzes 21 to 50, three points for each question answered correctly in Quizzes 51 to 80, four points for each question answered correctly in Quizzes 81 to 110, and five points for each question answered correctly in Quizzes 111 to 132. The best possible score in the Mastermind Challenge is therefore 4000, and if you achieve this you can consider yourself a true genius! A score of 2000 would be average, and 3000 excellent. Anything over 3000 makes you a Mastermind, and over 3500 makes you a Mega-mastermind!

The Trivia Subject Challenge

If you know your knowledge is particularly strong in certain areas and weak in others, try the Trivia

Subject Challenge. Work through the quizzes consecutively but start by answering just the questions on your particular subject. For example, if you are especially knowledgeable about natural history, work through the book answering all the question 7s first. Then go on to your next best subject and answer all the questions on that, then on to your next best, and so on, leaving the hardest questions till last. Award yourself one point for each question answered correctly in your first category, two points each for each question answered correctly in the next three categories, three points for each question answered correctly in the following three categories, four points for each question answered correctly in the following two categories, and five points for each question answered correctly in the final category. This gives you a possible score of 3828, and anyone who achieves it is also a genius! A score of 1900 would be average, and 2800 excellent. Over 2800 puts you in the Mastermind class, and over 3300 makes you a Mega-mastermind!

The Tricky Trivia Breakout

Tricky Trivia Breakout is a game for two to four players. All you need to play is the grid, which you will find overleaf, and a counter or coin for each player. If you only have one copy of the book between you then you will need either to tear out the page with the grid on it or trace it off or take a photocopy of it, which you may be able to do at the local library.

Each player starts with a coin or counter in one of the centre four squares, and to see who starts first, toss a coin or shake a die. The aim is to work through the squares by answering the quiz questions they refer to, until you reach the outside edge of the grid. Each square has a heavy black number, which is the number of the quiz, and a lighter number, which is the number of the question. For example, if you start at 1/8, you will have to answer the eighth question in the first quiz. When you have done that successfully, you then choose another square to move to, and you continue in this way, taking your turn with the other players, until one of you has reached the edge of the grid, the first person to do so being the winner. You can choose which way to work through the grid, but you can only move upwards, downwards, to the left or to the right, not diagonally. If you cannot answer a question, then you have to go back to the previous square and try moving out in a different direction when your turn comes next.

Each quiz is represented once in the grid, and there are examples of all kinds of questions, so you can try and find the easiest route for you. However, it is not possible to work your way out answering only one kind of question!

Whichever way you choose to work through the book, have fun, and don't be tempted to look at the answers in the back until you have finished.

Tricky Trivia Breakout Grid

				129/4	119/7	110/8	96/9					
			120/10	31/5	95/6	98/7	17/10	89/2				
		117/1	62/6	91/9	29/3	48/5	76/4	37/8	124/9			
	108/10	32/3	57/8	56/1	63/9	75/4	43/6	87/2	40/5	132/7		
	122/7	66/1	49/4	93/3	23/6	33/2	3/10	11/4	77/8	84/1	52/3	92/9
105/4	70/2	34/3	74/10	21/7	45/5	1/8	22/6	15/3	26/9	86/2	38/5	50/7	126/8
130/5	88/3	12/8	80/6	13/4	6/7	**START**	5/9	79/1	39/8	44/4	81/2	118/5
116/3	73/7	18/2	96/3	9/5	20/4		19/10	8/4	27/5	85/2	103/10	121/3
127/5	42/10	68/6	36/9	83/1	10/2	14/2	2/5	4/7	72/3	41/9	54/8	64/3	115/6
	104/2	60/4	71/7	58/8	24/2	7/10	46/7	35/9	47/6	102/4	69/10	125/1
		113/1	65/2	55/5	99/9	59/4	16/1	51/5	78/2	53/7	109/4	
			106/9	101/6	28/10	30/2	67/8	94/6	61/3	123/3		
				112/8	82/7	97/5	100/9	25/4	107/3			
				128/2	111/6	131/10	114/7					

THE QUIZZES

1

1. Which famous film was about a shark that terrorized holidaymakers in America?
2. An advocate is a kind of pear. True or false?
3. Where is the English Derby run?
4. What branch of science does botany deal with?
5. In which city is Kennedy Airport?
6. Whose hit was the 1984 record 'Wild Boys'?
7. How many legs has a spider?
8. Who wrote stories about Peter Rabbit?
9. Which member of the Royal Family left the Royal Marines in 1987?
10. What is a kayak?

WILD BOYS.
please do not feed.

1/6   A real hit?

2

1. The village of Beckindale is near which famous TV farm?
2. The Cheviot Hills are in Wales. True or false?
3. Which tennis player is known as 'Superbrat'?
4. Which gas do we need in order to breathe?
5. In which city might you see a gondola?
6. Which pop singer appeared in a TV ad for jeans?
7. What is a badger's burrow called?
8. Which city is the home of the Bolshoi Ballet?
9. Who was the first president of the USA?
10. When would you use the Green Cross Code?

3

1. Who is comedian Bobby Ball's partner?
2. Coral is produced by living creatures. True or false?
3. In which sport is Diego Maradona famous?
4. What colour are copper sulphate crystals?
5. Which English city is known for making cutlery?
6. In which band is Holly Johnson the lead singer?
7. What kind of tree produces acorns?
8. In which book by Daniel Defoe would you find Man Friday?
9. Which comedian used to say, 'Just like that!'?
10. Which is larger, a hectare or an acre?

4

1. Who is the star of *The Secret of My Success*?
2. Hollywood is part of San Francisco. True or false?
3. What game do the New York Yankees play?
4. What is a barometer used for?
5. Which river runs through London?
6. Who presents the Radio One *Breakfast Show*?
7. What are the seven colours of the rainbow?
8. Which musical instrument do you associate with Yehudi Menuhin?
9. How many husbands had Queen Elizabeth I?
10. Where can you see the Crown Jewels?

4/6   Morning all

5

1. Who, in early films, wore a bowler hat, striped trousers, carried a cane, and was known as the 'little fellow'?
2. Foxgloves are poisonous. True or false?
3. Which football team is known as the 'Swans'?
4. What connects the name 'Columbia' with space travel?
5. In which country would you use guilders as currency?
6. What kind of music is Nashville, Tennessee, known for?
7. Which kinds of birds coo?
8. La Scala is a building in Milan. What is it famous for?
9. For what achievement are Hillary and Tenzing famous?
10. What did the letters £ s d stand for?

6

1. How many dalmatians were there in the Disney cartoon?
2. The Great Wall of China can be seen from the moon. True or false?
3. Which city is host to the 1988 Olympic Games?
4. How many teeth does a human adult have?
5. What's the capital city of New Zealand?

6. On Mel and Kim's album 'FLM' what do the letters FLM stand for?
7. What is a dandie dinmont?
8. How many lines has a limerick?
9. Who was Charles de Gaulle?
10. Is Big Ben, in London, a clock, a bell, or a tower?

eating smiling whistling biting

6/4 Give us a smile

7

1. What is the flying cartoon teddy bear called?
2. Sri Lanka used to be called Siam. True or false?
3. Which female athlete is famous for running barefoot?
4. What kind of equipment has data buses, control buses and address buses?
5. Where are the Needles?
6. Which pop group wrote the second letter of its name backwards?
7. How does a fish breathe?
8. Who was Romeo's sweetheart?
9. Who was David Dimbleby's famous father?
10. Who was Prime Minister of Britain before Margaret Thatcher?

8

1. Of which pub in *EastEnders* is Dirty Den the landlord?
2. Snow is frozen rain. True or false?
3. What, in cricket, is a hat trick?
4. Where in the human body would you find a molar and an incisor?
5. Near which city is the palace of Versailles?
6. Who had a hit with 'A Little Boogie Woogie' in 1987?
7. In which part of the world would you find a penguin?
8. Who played croquet with hedgehogs and flamingos in a well-loved children's book?
9. Who was Al Capone?
10. Which country does moussaka come from?

8/3   A hat trick

9

1. What does Russell Grant do on television?
2. The River Rhône flows through Switzerland. True or false?

3. In which sport is the Ryder Cup awarded?
4. What do unlike poles of a magnet do?
5. By what name do English-speaking people know the city of Firenze?
6. Who had 'No Sleep Till Brooklyn'?
7. What are the cabbage white, the peacock and the tortoiseshell?
8. Who wrote the *Messiah*?
9. Who invented the telephone?
10. When was the Queen's Silver Jubilee: 1975, 1977 or 1979?

10

1. Who was *My Family and Other Animals* about?
2. Loch Lomond is the largest lake in Great Britain. True or false?
3. What has a boom, a jib and a centreboard?
4. What is the boiling point of water?
5. In which country is Antwerp?
6. What is the full title of this traditional song: 'Sweet Lass of _____ Hill' ?
7. What kind of cat has no tail?
8. Who were Porthos, Athos and Aramis?
9. Who was Butch Cassidy's friend and associate?
10. What colour is the District Line on a London Underground map?

11

1. Which TV serial, based on a book by Douglas Adams, had a character called Ford Prefect?
2. Yew trees are used to make longbows. True or false?
3. What sport takes place at Silverstone?
4. What is Charles Macintosh famous for?
5. Off the coast of which European country/countries is the Bay of Biscay?
6. Which reggae star sang 'No Woman No Cry'?
7. What kind of animals do Americans call cottontails?
8. Where in Britain are the Proms staged?
9. How did Joan of Arc die?
10. Which two British cities are connected by the A1?

11/7   A cottontail

12

1. Which days is *Wogan* on TV?
2. The Beaufort Scale is used to measure earthquakes. True or false?
3. Which stretch of water was Captain Matthew Webb the first man to swim?
4. What is sodium chloride better known as?
5. In which city can you see the Arc de Triomphe?
6. Which trio did Sting sing with?
7. Which of these birds migrate: blackbird, swallow, thrush?
8. Who wrote the Noddy books?
9. Whose wife was Guinevere?
10. What is the national airline of Ireland?

13

1. What appears on the *Blue Peter* emblem?
2. A tomato is a vegetable. True or false?
3. What are the All Blacks?
4. Who invented the steam engine?
5. Which is the Muslims' holy city?
6. Which song by Ben E. King is also the title of a film – the song is the theme tune?
7. What is an amphibian?
8. Which Dickens' character asked for more?
9. Which record producer and adventurer attempted to cross the Atlantic in a balloon?
10. What is the maximum speed allowed on Britain's motorways?

14

1. What was Superman's other name?
2. Two-thirds of the earth's surface is covered with water. True or false?
3. In which sport/sports would you use a 'rest'?
4. What sort of scientist would use the light year as a unit of measurement?
5. Which two continents are divided by the Bering Strait?
6. 'Who's That Girl?'
7. What is a Busy Lizzie?
8. Whose friend was Eeyore?
9. What business is Robert Maxwell mainly concerned with?
10. What kind of conveyance has a Plimsoll Line?

15

1. What did Wincey Willis do on TV-am?
2. A conga is a kind of snake. True or false?
3. What is the MCC?
4. What is H_2SO_4?
5. Which river flows over Victoria Falls?
6. Who is Reginald Dwight better known as?
7. Where would you find a stamen?
8. Which is the higher voice, soprano or contralto?
9. Of which country is Hirohito emperor?
10. What are Amtrack, BR and SNCF?

16

1. Who was the original film James Bond?
2. It is impossible to swallow and breathe at the same time. True or false?
3. With which sport is Michael Whitaker associated?
4. What is arthritis a disease of: the throat, the nose, the joints?
5. What is the biggest island in the world?
6. Whose guitarist is Robin Campbell?
7. What is the world's largest land bird?
8. In which pantomime does Buttons appear?
9. Who is the patron saint of animals?
10. What is tagliatelle?

16/7   A nice little feather boa

17

1. How does Anneka Rice travel around in *Treasure Hunt*?
2. Jane Austen wrote *Great Expectations*. True or false?
3. What kind of sportsman or woman might be a black belt?
4. What type of animal suckles its young?
5. What's the capital of Cuba?
6. Which birds 'cried' in the title of a Prince hit?
7. At what time of year do daffodils flower?
8. How many strings has a guitar: four, six or eight?
9. Which English king lost his jewels in the Wash?
10. Which much-loved royal lady has her birthday on 4 August?

18

1. Which actor who used to play the character of the Doctor in *Dr Who* died in 1987?
2. Rhubarb leaves are poisonous. True or false?
3. How many players are there in a rugby union team?
4. What was Yuri Gagarin's notable achievement in April 1961?
5. Which is further north, New York or Paris?
6. What is the name of the former Culture Club drummer who set up a group called Heartbeat UK?

7. What are hips and haws?
8. What does *forte* mean in music?
9. In the Bible, whose brother was Esau?
10. What's the name of the Prince and Princess of Wales's country house?

19/2 The Milky Bar Kit

19

1. Which film hero went to the Temple of Doom?
2. Cats only drink milk. True or false?
3. How long is a marathon?
4. Which chemical element is represented by the letters Fe?
5. Where are the Cambrian Mountains?
6. Which band does Chris Kavanagh belong to?
7. What is a percheron?
8. What is a lithograph?
9. Who said, 'Dr Livingstone, I presume'?
10. What is a gargoyle?

20

1. Who hosted *What's My Line?*
2. Fleas can jump 130 times their own height. True or false?
3. How many counters does each player have in draughts?
4. What colour does litmus paper turn when dipped into an alkaline solution: red, blue or purple?
5. Which is in the southern hemisphere, the Tropic of Cancer or the Tropic of Capricorn?
6. Which pop hero was 'Born to Run'?
7. What is the Milky Way?
8. Who is Joan Sutherland?
9. Who built the locomotive called the 'Rocket'?
10. How many days does Lent last?

20/6   Born to run

21

1. Which famous comic actor played Inspector Clouseau in the *Pink Panther* films?
2. Adolphe Sax invented the saxophone. True or false?

3. Which football team is known as the Blades?
4. By what name is acetic acid better known?
5. In which group of islands are St Mary's,
   St Martin's, Tresco and Bryher?
6. What is the title of Michael Jackson's world
   best-selling album which came out in 1982?
7. What is the chameleon noted for?
8. Who painted the Mona Lisa?
9. Which king of England commanded the
   waves to go back?
10. What do the German words *damen* and
    herren mean?

22

1. On which best-selling book is Roy Castle's
   Record Breakers show based?
2. Edinburgh is on the Firth of Tay. True or
   false?
3. Who won the 1987 FA Cup Final?
4. How often does Halley's Comet return to
   earth?
5. Where is Alice Springs?
6. 'Come into the garden, _____ .'
   To whom was the invitation issued in the
   Victorian song?
7. Which bird's song is said to resemble, 'A
   little bit of bread and no cheese'?
8. Whose butler was Jeeves?
9. Which famous French hero died in exile on
   St Helena?
10. What is bouillabaisse?

23

1. Which actor played Crocodile Dundee?
2. A Pomeranian is a breed of cat. True or false?
3. How many clubs are there in a set of golf clubs?
4. Approximately how fast does Concorde fly: 1000mph (1610 km/h), 1500mph (2414 km/h), or 2000mph (3220 km/h)?
5. In which European city would you find O'Connell Street?
6. Which popular musical was based on a book by the poet T. S. Eliot?
7. How many birds have teeth?
8. Whose painting of sunflowers achieved a record price in March 1987?
9. What nationality is Sophia Loren, the famous film star?
10. What are Minton, Wedgwood and Crown Derby?

24

1. What are Cagney and Lacey's first names?
2. You can tell the age of a horse by its teeth. True or false?
3. How often are the Commonwealth Games held?
4. What forms the 'brain' of a robot?
5. Where is Stonehenge?

6. Who, according to the LP, had a 'Lonely Hearts Club Band'?
7. What kind of tree produces conkers?
8. How many lines has a sonnet?
9. Who used to be married to the Earl of Snowdon?
10. What might be size A3, A4 or A5?

25

1. Which TV channel recently serialized *Oliver Twist*?
2. Dr Jekyll and Mr Hyde were the same person. True or false?
3. What do people do with 'clay pigeons'?
4. Is the Royal Greenwich Observatory in Greenwich?
5. What's the capital of Poland?
6. What do Janice Long and Anne Nightingale have in common?
7. What is a begonia?
8. Which famous literary family, authors of books like *Jane Eyre* and *Wuthering Heights*, lived in the West Yorkshire village of Haworth?
9. Whom is Lee Harvey Oswald believed to have murdered?
10. What is a mantilla: is it a Spanish dance, a Spanish scarf or a kind of wine?

26

1. What have these films in common: *The Sting, Winning* and *The Colour of Money*?
2. There are 617 known species of spiders in Britain. True or false?
3. The modern pentathlon comprises five sports. What are they?
4. Who was the first man on the moon?
5. Which London street is associated with doctors?
6. Which *EastEnders* star had a hit with 'Every Loser Wins'?
7. What kind of animal is a leveret?
8. Brahms, Picasso, Vivaldi — which is the odd man out?
9. What connects Sir Christopher Wren with St Paul's Cathedral in London?
10. What is a courgette?

27

1. What creatures did Mr Spock and Co. try to save in *Star Trek IV*?
2. Henry VIII had eight wives. True or false?
3. What is Jo Durie's sport?
4. What are FORTH, FORTRAN and COBOL?
5. Where is the National Exhibition Centre?
6. Which star's hair caught fire when he made a Pepsi-Cola advert in 1984?
7. What jewel comes from oysters?
8. Whose arch enemy was Professor Moriarty

in the famous mystery books by Sir Arthur
Conan Doyle?
9. Who was Homer?
10. What is the French national anthem called?

26/4   Welcome to the Space Age Burger Bar

28

1. Who were Harpo, Groucho and Chico?
2. The capital of Australia is Sydney. True or false?
3. What sport takes place at Trent Bridge?
4. What can you pick up with a magnet?
5. Where in London is Poets' Corner?
6. Who is George O'Dowd better known as?
7. What colour eyes do Siamese cats have?
8. Which king of Scotland gave his name to a play by Shakespeare?
9. Who lives in the Vatican?
10. What is New York's Broadway known for?

29

1. Which TV school do Fay and Hollo attend?
2. A doublet was a Spanish gold coin. True or false?
3. Which football team is called the Peacocks?
4. What colour is a sapphire?
5. In which European city is Orly Airport?
6. Whose first hit was 'Mandy'?
7. What is a female sheep called?
8. Who lived at Green Gables?
9. Who is Jeffrey Archer?
10. What is 0.75 as a fraction?

30

1. In which film did Dudley Moore play Patch the Elf?
2. Bees collect honey. True or false?
3. What kind of sporting activity takes place on the Pennine Way?
4. Which is the odd man out: lead, mercury, tin?
5. Which street in New York is famous for its financial wheeling and dealing?
6. Which pop star's daughter is called Fifi Trixibelle?
7. What colour is a female blackbird?
8. Who wrote the 'New World' symphony?
9. Of which European country is Baudouin king?
10. What are cornflakes made from?

31

1. Which actor plays Terry in *Minder*?
2. 16°C equals 61°F. True or false?
3. Who was world champion racing driver in 1986?
4. What do decibels measure?
5. Who lives at 11 Downing Street?
6. From which country did the original members of the band AC/DC come?
7. Is a dolphin a fish?
8. What was Michelangelo famous for?
9. Who 'looked out on the feast of Stephen'?
10. Which day of the week is the Jewish sabbath?

31/9   The feast of Stephen

32

1. Which precious stone is missing from this film's title: *The _____ Forest*?
2. A human being has thirty bones in each arm. True or false?
3. In which sport would you use a puck?
4. In which fresh foods would you find citric acid?
5. Which Italian city has a famous leaning tower?
6. Who sang 'Lady in Red'?
7. Which beetle, named after an American State, must be reported to the police if seen in Britain?
8. Who was Piet Mondrian?
9. Of which country was Mao-tse Tung leader in the 1950s and 1960s?
10. When is All Saints' Day?

33

1. Who played Adrian Mole in the TV series?
2. Margaret Thatcher is MP for Grantham. True or false?
3. With which sport is Dennis Lillee associated?
4. What, in chemistry, is a retort?
5. Where is the Golden Gate Bridge?
6. Which band does Midge Ure lead?
7. Why do spiders spin webs?
8. Which is the odd one out: flute, trumpet, oboe, bassoon?

9. What weapon was invented by Samuel Colt?
10. What year was the Falklands War?

34

1. Who, with Penfold, foiled the evil schemes of Baron Greenback?
2. Gorillas have been known to live for over fifty years in captivity. True or false?
3. Which champion boxer was known as the 'Louisville Lip'?
4. Which two numbers are used in the binary system?
5. Is the German Democratic Republic East Germany or West Germany?
6. Who sang 'Sweet Sixteen'?
7. What is the world's fastest land animal?
8. What was Henry Moore's art?
9. What is Marcel Marceau famous for?
10. What is mah jong — a martial art, a food, or a game?

32/7   Beware the Beetle

35

1. What is Taggart's job in the TV series?
2. It is easier to float than to sink in the Dead Sea. True or false?
3. What is the A.A.A.?
4. Which gas smells like rotten eggs?
5. In which British city is the Royal Mile?
6. Which pop group played 'The Game'?
7. What kind of animal is a basenji?
8. Who wrote a piano sonata known as the Moonlight Sonata?
9. What did Sir Robert Peel found?
10. What, in the newspaper world, is Reuters?

35/5   The Royal Mile

36

1. Who were Graham Chapman, John Cleese, Terry Gilliam, Eric Idle, Terry Jones and Michael Palin?

2. The South American giant frog can fly. True or false?
3. What is the Cresta Run?
4. What speed is Mach 1? Is it approximately 1200 km/h (750mph), 1600 km/h (1000mph) or 2000 km/h (1250mph)?
5. Where is England's longest road bridge?
6. Which group is named after a drink made from orange juice and champagne?
7. What is a cygnet?
8. In which ballet does the Sugar Plum Fairy appear?
9. Who invented the ballpoint pen?
10. What kind of dog is Snoopy?

37

1. Which two TV reporters go in at the deep end?
2. In 1647 the English parliament abolished Christmas. True or false?
3. What game do the Harlem Globe Trotters play?
4. Which precious metal has the chemical symbol Au?
5. Which is the largest ocean in the world?
6. Which group did Jody Watley sing with?
7. Where do swallows fly to in autumn?
8. In which branch of the arts were Reynolds and Gainsborough distinguished?
9. For which English king was the Royal Pavilion in Brighton built?
10. Who would wear a kimono?

38

1. What is the complete title of this film: *Close Encounters of the* _____ *Kind*?
2. There are more miles of canals in Birmingham than in Venice. True or false?
3. What are Newmarket and Old Maid?
4. What did Wilhelm Röntgen discover?
5. Where is Kingsford Smith Airport?
6. Who sang a pop song about Michael Caine?
7. From which fish does caviare come?
8. What in the musical world is the E.N.O.?
9. Charles Babbage invented the forerunner of a device considered indispensable in the modern world. What is it?
10. What is porridge made from?

39

1. Whose arch enemy was Scunner Campbell?
2. In Burma people gamble on the results of fish-fighting contests. True or false?
3. Who won the 1987 Derby?
4. Which famous Second World War weapon did Barnes Wallis invent?
5. Which part of England is known as the Black Country?
6. What kind of music does Aretha Franklin sing?
7. What is a slow worm?
8. Doh, ray, me, fah, soh, _____, te, doh. What is missing?

9. Which modern invention did John Logie Baird pioneer?
10. What is a piece of land surrounded by water called?

40

1. Who is *The Tube*'s male presenter?
2. Humming-birds can fly backwards. True or false?
3. Which football team's home ground is Goodison Park?
4. In which science was Pythagoras distinguished?
5. Where is the Giant's Causeway?
6. Which pop singer had a yacht called *Drum* which collapsed in the Fastnet race?
7. Which animals can suffer from myxomatosis?
8. Who was Anna Pavlova?
9. Which English king was called Prince Hal before he was sovereign?
10. Which English admiral sailed in the *Victory*?

39/7   A slow worm?

41

1. Who is Ian McCaskill?
2. In 1979 snow fell in the Sahara Desert. True or false?
3. How many players are there in a hockey team?
4. After whom is the unit of electric current named?
5. Where in Great Britain are Rum, Eigg and Muck?
6. Harry Webb has been a pop star for over twenty years. By what name is he better known?
7. From the wood of which trees are cricket bats made?
8. Picasso, Manet, Bizet, Goya – who is the odd man out?
9. Who reputedly rode a horse naked through the streets of Coventry?
10. What is the R.N.L.I.?

42

1. In which TV series was there a quick-tempered vet called Siegfried?
2. Victor Hugo was a famous American writer. True or false?
3. What sport do people play with large stones on ice?
4. Who discovered penicillin?
5. What is the Taj Mahal?

6. Where did the Proclaimers hope for a letter from?
7. Which disease killed thousands of elm trees in the 1970s?
8. Who is Bryony Brind? Is she a soprano, a violinist or a ballet dancer?
9. Which English king was killed at the Battle of Bosworth Field?
10. On what form of transport would you find a derailleur?

43

1. Who presents *Crimewatch*?
2. A gingko is a kind of large lizard. True or false?
3. Who was the only British gold medallist in the 1987 World Athletics Championships?
4. Which part of the body does bronchitis affect?
5. What is England's highest mountain?
6. Which British pop group, named after the official Unemployment Benefit card, visited the U.S.S.R. in 1986?
7. What kind of creature might be a cob or a pen?
8. Which great classical guitarist died in June 1987?
9. Who was Boudicca or Boadicea?
10. Where might you suffer from *mal de mer*?

45/10   A jet propelled sporran?

44

1. Which was the second 'Star Wars' movie?
2. No piece of paper can be folded in half more than seven times. True or false?
3. What is a point to point?
4. What is an electron?
5. Where is Sugar Loaf Mountain?
6. What, in the song, did Old Macdonald have?
7. In which country might you see a wombat?
8. In which book did Wendy, John and Michael Darling appear?
9. Who was murdered in Canterbury Cathedral in 1170?
10. By what name is an 'equine quadruped' better known?

45

1. Which TV quiz show is presented by Bob Holness?

2. The bat is the only mammal that can fly. True or false?
3. In which sport is the Londonderry Cup awarded?
4. What is a 'user-friendly' computer program?
5. In which sea bordering Britain is the Dogger Bank?
6. Which female singer dressed as Elvis Presley at a Grammy ceremony?
7. What are teal, mallard and widgeon?
8. Who wrote *Charlie and the Chocolate Factory*?
9. Who led Britain's Labour Party before Neil Kinnock?
10. What was the Flying Scotsman?

46

1. Which *EastEnders* character owns a pug called Willy?
2. A delphinium is a tall red flower. True or false?
3. When does the British football season start?
4. What is meant by the force of gravity?
5. Where is the Yellowstone National Park?
6. In which American city did Motown originate?
7. What is a marsupial?
8. What was Edward Lear famous for?
9. Whose wife, according to the Bible, was turned into a pillar of salt?
10. Where might you find a 'greyhound' that has wheels and an engine?

47

1. Who is the cartoon character Tom is always chasing?
2. Spiders' webs used to be used on wounds to stop them bleeding. True or false?
3. What sport do Juventus play?
4. Who invented the diesel engine?
5. What condiment is the French city of Dijon famous for?
6. What were the first names of Duran Duran's three Taylors?
7. Which wild creatures are famous for living on the Rock of Gibraltar?
8. Which Gilbert and Sullivan opera bears the name of a ship?
9. Which English king supposedly burnt the cakes?
10. What does BMX stand for?

48

1. Who starred in *Beverly Hills Cop*?
2. A marmoset is a set of marmalade jars. True or false?
3. In which sport do the Queensberry Rules apply?
4. When were the first landings on Mars made: 1970, 1976 or 1986?
5. What are Hokkaido, Honshu, Shikoku and Kyushu?

6. Which instrument did the famous jazz musician Louis Armstrong play?
7. How many arms has a starfish?
8. Who created *The Snowman*?
9. Which English monarch's favourite was the Earl of Essex?
10. Which two European countries are connected by the Mont Blanc tunnel?

49

1. Which crazy 'Carry On' film was set in ancient Egypt?
2. If you travel from east to west across the Soviet Union you cross seven time zones. True or false?
3. Which snooker player wears upside-down glasses?
4. What kind of equipment contains silicon chips?
5. In which country is Mount Ararat?
6. Which two stars made a version of 'Dancing in the Street' and appeared on video at the Live Aid concert?
7. Which is the most common blood group?
8. Which great Austrian composer wrote the operas *The Magic Flute* and *The Marriage of Figaro*?
9. After whom was the teddy bear named?
10. Where in the USA is the NASA mission control centre?

50

1. Where did Superman originally come from?
2. Every snowflake has a different pattern. True or false?
3. What is the Milk Race?
4. What do the letters ROM stand for in computer language?
5. What's the capital of Denmark?
6. Which Norwegian band is made up of Morten, Mags and Pal?
7. What is lichen?
8. Who wrote the Brandenburg Concertos?
9. Which famous naval hero's mistress was Lady Hamilton?
10. Which motorway runs between Hull and Liverpool?

51

1. What kind of animal is Mister Ed?
2. The Tower of London was built in the reign of Queen Victoria. True or false?
3. How long is a cricket bail?
4. What is the speed of light?
5. Where is the Zuider Zee?
6. Which city did the Beatles come from?
7. What kind of plant is the 'death cap'?
8. Who was George Eliot?
9. What is Harold Pinter famous for?
10. What do Americans mean by a 'sidewalk'?

52

1. Whose catchphrase is, 'It's the way I tell 'em.'?
2. John Lennon's middle name was Winston. True or false?
3. Who is the only horse to have won the Grand National three times?
4. What do ornithologists study?
5. In which South American country is the Orinoco river?
6. Who was 'Incommunicado'?
7. Which is the longest-lived mammal excluding man?
8. What connects the play *Pygmalion* with the film/musical *My Fair Lady*?
9. What was Princess Diana's name before she became Princess of Wales?
10. What follows red in the traffic lights sequence?

50/3   A lotta bottle!

53

1. Who is TV-am's exercise queen?
2. Kangaroos are only about 1 centimetre (half an inch) long at birth. True or false?
3. What do the five interlocked Olympic rings represent?
4. What is haemoglobin?
5. What do English-speaking people call the city of München?
6. 'Ding dong bell.' Who was in the well?
7. What kind of creature is a mollusc?
8. Vanessa, Lynn and Corin are three members of a famous theatrical family. What is their surname?
9. Who was Britain's first prime minister?
10. Chatsworth House is a stately home. In which county is it?

54

1. Where might you see Louise Burton as a kennel maid?
2. Spartan, Blenheim and russet are types of pear. True or false?
3. Who, between 1965 and 1973, won twenty-seven Grand Prix motor races?
4. Which gas do plants breathe in the daytime?
5. In which English county is Chesil Beach?
6. Which pop duo were invited to perform in Peking in 1987?
7. What is a burbot?

8. Which famous German composer is associated with Bayreuth?
9. Which famous twin of a famous mother married a Texan heiress in February 1987?
10. What do the letters of 'radar' stand for?

53/2   A very little bouncing baby

55

1. Who are Hannibal, Faceman, Murdock and Baracus?
2. George I of England could neither speak nor write English. True or false?
3. What is Steve Lundquist's sport?
4. How big is the human heart? Is it about the size of your foot, the size of your fist, or the size of your ear?
5. Off which continent is the island of Tasmania?
6. How is Christopher Hamill better known?
7. What kind of plant is pennyroyal?
8. Who is the Poet Laureate?
9. When did Guy Fawkes set up the Gunpowder Plot? Was it in 1605, 1625 or 1635?
10. What would you do with pumpernickel?

56

1. Who presented *Mooncat & Co*?
2. All worker bees are male. True or false?
3. Which sport takes place at Gleneagles?
4. What is the freezing point of water?
5. Where is Palermo: in Argentina, Sicily or Indonesia?
6. Who sang a pop song about Robert De Niro?
7. Which is the odd snake out: anaconda, cobra, python?
8. In which Shakespearian play did Ophelia appear?
9. In which country did the outlaw Ned Kelly operate?
10. What colour is indigo?

57/1   A pecking pain?

57

1. Which comedian has an ostrich companion?
2. Once they have been picked, oranges cease to ripen. True or false?

3. What does 'bowling a maiden over' mean in cricket?
4. What is the largest single organ in the human body? (N.B. You can see it!)
5. In which country is Baghdad?
6. Which honour did the Queen bestow on Bob Geldof in 1986?
7. What is the largest wild mammal in Britain?
8. Who wrote stories about the 'Scarlet Pimpernel'?
9. What were William Burke and William Hare famous for: inventing, politics or crime?
10. Which country does Gorgonzola cheese come from?

58

1. What's the name of 'the world's first computer-generated TV show host'?
2. A differential on a car powers the lights. True or false?
3. What is Graham Dilley's sport?
4. What did William Harvey discover about the human body?
5. Of which city is Manhattan a part?
6. Who sang 'Mull of Kintyre'?
7. What is the small ornamental Chinese carp better known as?
8. Who was Titania?
9. Who was the English nurse famous for her work among the casualties of the Crimean War?
10. Who killed Goliath?

59

1. Who was James Bond's boss?
2. Each day about ten million people celebrate the same birthday. True or false?
3. Where are the highest waves found for surf riding – Australia, California or Hawaii?
4. Who invented the hovercraft?
5. Corsica and Sardinia are both Mediterranean islands. Which is farther north?
6. Which pop group had a lead singer called Morrisey?
7. When should you *not* feed birds?
8. Which Welsh poet wrote *Under Milk Wood*?
9. Who was Fletcher Christian?
10. When was the Battle of Agincourt: 1215, 1315 or 1415?

60

1. Which aristocratic detective featured in a number of TV serials with a character called Harriet Vane?
2. A person's largest muscles are in their buttocks. True or false?
3. Who was the 1987 world snooker champion?
4. What does a tachograph measure?
5. Where is the Weddell Sea: Antarctica, Australasia or the Middle East?
6. Which musical does Elaine Page's and

Barbara Dickson's song 'I Know Him So Well' come from?

7. What kind of animal is called ermine when it gets its white winter coat?
8. What is the longest-running play on the London stage?
9. Which of the Queen's sons is called Philip Arthur George after his first name?
10. Which is heavier, milk or cream?

61

1. What was the Crossroads in the former TV series?
2. A pike is a large sea fish. True or false?
3. Who captained the English cricket team in the First Test against Pakistan in 1987?
4. Which parts of the body are called cervical, thoracic and lumbar?
5. Which two countries does St George's Channel separate?
6. Who, in the song, killed Cock Robin?
7. From which trees' wood were bows for archery made?
8. In which Dickens' novel does Uriah Heep appear?
9. When was Edward VIII king of England: 1926, 1936 or 1946?
10. What is a Lamborghini?

62

1. Which was the dreadful girls' school about which a number of very funny films were made in the 1950s?
2. The most northerly town in the world is Hammerfest in Norway. True or false?
3. What kind of sportsman would use an iron, a putter or a wood?
4. After which American president is the Space Center at Cape Canaveral in Florida, USA, named?
5. Where is Madagascar?
6. Who had 'a little red Corvette'?
7. What are Etna, Vesuvius and Mauna Loa?
8. What was George Stubbs famous for?
9. Who was Ovid: a painter, a sculptor or a poet?
10. Who, or what, is the Old Lady of Threadneedle Street?

63

1. *The Magnificent* _____ — what number is missing from the title of this classic Western?

2. The Isle of Skye is off the northern coast of Scotland. True or false?
3. What was Emerson Fittipaldi's sport?
4. What is the lowest prime number?
5. Where are the Atlas Mountains: Switzerland, Morocco or Brazil?
6. Who presents ITV's pop show *The Roxy*?
7. The Marianas Trench is the deepest part of any ocean in the world. In which ocean is it?
8. Who wrote *The Secret Garden*?
9. Which female member of the Royal Family gained a pilot's licence in 1987?
10. Who betrayed Jesus for thirty pieces of silver?

64

1. Which TV star says, 'Come on down, the price is right.'?
2. Biggles was a famous Second World War flying ace. True or false?
3. What do you play shinty with?
4. In what year did man first stand on the moon: 1949, 1959 or 1969?
5. Where is Speakers' Corner?
6. Who made the 'Graceland' LP?
7. Which sparrow has a black 'bib' – the male or the female?
8. What kind of instruments are triangles, castanets and tambourines?
9. A famous literary character was modelled on Alice Liddell. Who was she?
10. Which is longer, a metre or a yard?

65

1. What was BBC TV's holiday camp series called?
2. Admiral Nelson suffered from seasickness. True or false?
3. What sporting event takes place at Henley?
4. With which railway company was Isambard Kingdom Brunel associated?
5. Which island's chief town is called St Peter Port?
6. How is Reginald Dwight better known?
7. What is measured on the Richter Scale?
8. Of which form of the arts was Sarah Bernhardt part?
9. Which American statesman and philosopher invented the lightning conductor?
10. Which two English words end in 'shion'?

66

1. Who starred in *Up the Elephant and Round the Castle*?
2. Napoleon is believed to have been killed by his wallpaper. True or false?
3. What connects John Anthony Curry with Jayne Torvill and Christopher Dean?
4. What nationality was the first woman astronaut?
5. In which European city is the Cathedral of Notre Dame?

6. Which Spanish singer played football with Real Madrid?
7. What kind of creature is a pipistrelle?
8. What is a theatre's green room?
9. Who is the astronomer who appears on TV?
10. How many notes are there in an octave?

67

1. In which film, starring Michael J. Fox, did crazy inventor Doc Brown invent a time machine?
2. Cats spend two-thirds of their lives asleep. True or false?
3. What kind of sporting event is the Calgary Stampede?
4. In which computer language can you PEEK and POKE?
5. Which is nearer to Australia, New Zealand or New Guinea?
6. 'It's Better To _____ ' – what's the title of this album by Swing Out Sister ?
7. What is permafrost?
8. Where in London is Shakespeare performed in the open air in the summer?
9. Who is married to John McEnroe?
10. Who or what lives in an apiary?

68

1. What are the names of the Grants' children in *Brookside*?
2. Yew trees can live for over 1000 years. True or false?
3. How many points are required to win a game of table tennis?
4. Which metal does the chemical symbol Cu stand for?
5. In which famous London cathedral is the Whispering Gallery?
6. What was Elvis Presley's first UK hit record: 'Blue Suede Shoes', 'Heartbreak Hotel' or 'Jailhouse Rock'?
7. Which is the world's largest sea bird?
8. What does a choreographer do?
9. Who wrote the novel *The Thirty-nine Steps*?
10. What does Cantab. stand for?

68/5   The Whispering Gallery

69

1. Which TV programme featured Dunmore United Football Club?
2. Caruso was a great Italian dancer. True or false?

3. Which American motor racing circuit is known as the Brickyard?
4. What is a hologram?
5. Which mountains run down the eastern side of the USA – the Rockies, the Appalachians or the Andes?
6. Which pop star's wife was Alana Hamilton?
7. What is, or are, krill?
8. What is an Eisteddfod?
9. Which game do Kasparov and Karpov play?
10. In 1987's Royal Grand Knockout Tournament on TV, whose team won?

70

1. *Desperately Seeking* ____ – what was the name of the film and which pop star appeared in it?
2. Ostrich racing is a popular sport in South Africa. True or false?
3. Who would use a crampon: a golf player, a snooker player or a mountaineer?
4. Cobalt, nickel, brass – which is the odd one out?
5. Which two countries border the Caspian Sea?
6. Which band took its name from a poster advertising a Frank Sinatra concert?
7. What are forsythia, kerria and syringa?
8. Who wrote *The Importance of Being Earnest*?
9. Whose daughter was Elizabeth I?
10. In which British city are Victoria and Piccadilly railway stations?

71

1. How many people are there in each of the *Call My Bluff* teams?
2. The Roman emperor Caligula made his horse a senator. True or false?
3. In which sport or sports could you follow a slalom course?
4. What does a prism do?
5. In which English county is the Cheddar Gorge?
6. Who sang the theme song of the film *Absolute Beginners*?
7. What would you do with a pawpaw?
8. Which Russian composer wrote the music for *Swan Lake*?
9. Who was Franklin Delano Roosevelt?
10. What are Watling Street and the Fosse Way?

72

1. Who has a *Madhouse*?
2. All Ford Granada cars are white. True or false?
3. If a cricket umpire put both arms up in the air, what would it signal?
4. Which heavenly body controls the tides on earth?
5. In which American state are the Everglades?
6. With which group did Michael Jackson originally sing?

7. What kinds of plant are timothy, rye and cocksfoot?
8. Which is the main home of opera and ballet in London?
9. What would you associate with Arthur Negus?
10. Which three colours are the French flag?

72/3   Hands up!

73

1. Who was Tonto?
2. Ice-cream was invented in 1620. True or false?
3. How many players are there in a netball team?
4. What is significant about the temperature $-273°C$?
5. Which two countries does Hadrian's Wall separate?
6. Who made 'Nikita' a hit in 1985?
7. Which bird is the national emblem of the USA?
8. What is meant by 'perspective' in drawing or painting?
9. Who was king of England before Victoria?
10. Where is Winston Churchill buried?

74

1. Which popular film character was asked to 'phone home'?
2. Eggs help cakes to rise. True or false?
3. Which equestrian sport shows the absolute obedience of the horse to the rider's signals?
4. Which is the hottest part of a Bunsen burner?
5. On which of the American Great Lakes is Toronto: Erie, Superior or Ontario?
6. In which American city was the American half of the Live Aid concert staged?
7. By which name is an antirrhinum better known?
8. What is Equity?
9. What was George Gershwin famous for?
10. What are the Cheyennes?

75

1. What's the pub in *Coronation Street* called?
2. An Alsatian's sense of smell is a million times better than a man's. True or false?
3. What is the Fosbury Flop?
4. By what name is the disease rubella better known?
5. Where would you spend an escudo?
6. What connects Alison Moyet with Yazoo?
7. In which part of the world would you find a llama?
8. Who wrote an Unfinished Symphony?

9. What was Maximilien Robespierre a leader of?
10. What does the Latin phrase *in situ* mean?

76

1. Where did Dracula live?
2. The word 'robot' comes from the Czech word *robota*. True or false?
3. Where is the Grand National run?
4. What is meant by organic chemistry?
5. Where would you be if you landed at Schiphol Airport?
6. Who are Will Sergeant, Les Pattinson, Ian McCulloch and Pete de Freitas?
7. Which has larger ears, an African elephant or an Indian elephant?
8. With which cities is the Halle Orchestra associated?
9. Which TV personality's wife is Lady Carina Fitzalan-Howard?
10. What is the standard gauge of railway line in Great Britain?

75/2 A supersensitive sniffer?

77

1. What is the complete title of the film *Greystoke*?
2. The Queen is not allowed in the House of Commons. True or false?
3. How many feathers can there be on a shuttlecock?
4. What does the chemical symbol S stand for?
5. Where are Sandown, Shanklin and Ventnor?
6. Who sang 'Keep Me In Mind'?
7. Which hang downwards from the roofs of caves, stalactites or stalagmites?
8. Which famous Greek-American soprano died in 1977?
9. Who were the four founder members of the SDP in Britain?
10. The Spirit of St Louis was a famous aircraft. Why was it famous?

78

1. In which TV series did Joanna Lumley play a character called Purdy?
2. Gentians are yellow flowers found in marshy areas. True or false?
3. Who achieved an amazing win in the Decathlon in Los Angeles in 1984?
4. Approximately how many bones are there in the human body — 100, 150 or 200?
5. Which famous European city has a bridge called the Bridge of Sighs?

6. What movie did the hit song 'The Heat Is On' come from?
7. What kind of bird lays its eggs in other birds' nests?
8. Of which opera company is Glasgow the headquarters?
9. Who was Henry VIII's first wife?
10. What, in Paris, is the Metro?

Registered Egg minder.

78/7 ??????

79

1. Who presents *Newsround*?
2. The 'wand' that shop assistants pass over the bar code on certain products is a laser. True or false?
3. What is Yiannis Kouros's sport?
4. On which animals did Pavlov perform his experiments on reflex action?
5. In which British city is Sauciehall Street?
6. Who sang with the Banshees?
7. Why is the death's head hawk moth so named?
8. Who wrote the poem about daffodils that begins 'I wandered lonely as a cloud'?
9. Who was Yoko Ono married to?
10. What does an aircraft's 'black box' do?

80

1. What was unusual about the film *The Tales of Beatrix Potter*?
2. Koala bears only eat the leaves of the eucalyptus tree. True or false?
3. When was boardsailing or windsurfing introduced into the Olympic Games: 1976, 1980 or 1984?
4. What was Copernicus the first man to do?
5. On which river is Leicester?
6. Who was 'A Boy from Nowhere'?
7. What is a Suffolk Punch?
8. What happens at Glyndebourne?
9. To which king of France was Marie Antoinette married?
10. What do Americans call petrol?

80/7   A real country bump'in!

81

1. Whose catchphrase is 'Fan, dabi, dozi'?
2. Black snow fell in Sweden in 1969. True or false?

3. Boris Becker was the youngest ever men's Wimbledon champion when he won in 1985. What was also surprising about his achievement in that year?
4. Which Greek mathematician was known as the 'father of geometry'?
5. Which is further north, Aberdeen or Inverness?
6. Which group made the highly successful album 'Band on the Run'?
7. Which is the world's largest mammal?
8. Who painted the *Laughing Cavalier*?
9. Who was Sir Edmund Halley?
10. What is the Queen's yacht called?

82

1. Who is the chairman of *Babble*?
2. Peach Melba is a dessert made with peaches and caramel. True or false?
3. Who scored the fastest-ever World Cup goal for England in Bilbao, 1982 — was it Kevin Keegan, Bryan Robson or Norman Whiteside?
4. Who invented the jet engine?
5. What is the capital of Canada?
6. With whom did Tina Turner perform at the Live Aid concert?
7. Where do housemartins nest?
8. What kind of paintings are housed in London's Tate Gallery?
9. Whose daughter is Zara Phillips?
10. Which British motor racing ace was killed in an air crash?

83

1. Which TV programme stars Bungle, George and Zippy?
2. A black widow is a kind of scorpion. True or false?
3. Which woman tennis champion won six Wimbledon singles titles, ten women's doubles titles and four mixed doubles titles?
4. What does an angström measure?
5. Which French town became a centre for sick people to visit on pilgrimage after St Bernadette claimed to have seen visions there?
6. Who composed the *Chariots of Fire* theme music?
7. What do herons eat?
8. What is Sir Godfrey Kneller famous for?
9. Which English king had a minstrel called Blondel?
10. What is unusual about David Blunkett, MP?

84

1. Which cartoon character says 'What's up, Doc?'?
2. Father Brown was a Roman Catholic priest-detective in stories by G. K. Chesterton. True or false?
3. What two nationalities are the holders of the world weightlifting records?

4. In which branch of science was Linnaeus distinguished?
5. Where is the Place de la Concorde?
6. With which religion is reggae music associated?
7. Which of these birds eat worms: sparrows, blue tits, blackbirds?
8. Which British composer wrote the operas *Peter Grimes, Albert Herring* and *Billy Budd*?
9. Which English king ordered the compilation of the Domesday Book?
10. Where does a car with a CH plate come from?

85

1. Who was Adrian Mole's girlfriend?
2. Ostriches can swim. True or false?
3. In which sport do the following categories apply: free, standard, rapid fire, centre fire, Olympic trap and Olympic skeet?
4. Who invented the vacuum flask?
5. Where is Madison Square Garden?
6. Which rock star appeared in chewing-gum and underwear ads?
7. What were beagle dogs bred to hunt?
8. What did Othello do to Desdemona in Shakespeare's play?
9. Who was Britain's youngest cabinet minister – and a former Labour prime minister?
10. Where would you expect to see the letters R.S.V.P.?

86

1. What was the first Indiana Jones film called?
2. Malawi used to be called Nyasaland. True or false?
3. What's the fastest a man has skiied downhill – is it 193 km/h (120mph); 209 km/h (130mph); or 216 km/h (135mph)?
4. What is the pancreas?
5. Where is the Isle of Dogs?
6. Which band welcomed listeners to the Pleasure Dome?
7. What kind of animal was Tarka in Harold Williamson's book?
8. What does 'libretto' mean?
9. Who, according to history, was inspired by a spider?
10. Of which religious institution are the dean and chapter the governing body?

87

1. What is Dame Edna Everage's real name?
2. A 'Tin Lizzie' was a soldier's metal mug. True or false?
3. In which winter sport is the Stanley Cup awarded?
4. Which is Concorde's fastest time between New York and London: under two hours, under three hours or under four hours?
5. In which country might you see a Mountie?

6. An ex-plumber, his first record was 'Sadie the Cleaning Lady', and he's now one of the biggest rock stars in Australia. Who is he?
7. What is the heaviest insect found in Britain?
8. Which opera, set in ancient Egypt, was performed there in 1987?
9. Which English king was beheaded in 1649?
10. What kind of animal was Rudyard Kipling's Maltese Cat?

88

1. Whose dog is Schnorbitz?
2. There are no rivers in Saudi Arabia. True or false?
3. Which football team is known as the Bulls?
4. A space probe named after an Italian artist came within a few hundred kilometres of Halley's Comet in 1986. What was its name?
5. Near which British city is the road network known as Spaghetti Junction?
6. Who was 'Serious'?
7. What is notable about the stonefish?
8. In which Gilbert and Sullivan opera is there a 'very model of a modern major-general'?
9. Who is Karol Wojtyla better known as?
10. Which English football team plays in the Scottish Football League?

89

1. Who is Fievel Mousekewitz?
2. Winston Churchill was born in a chaplain's bedroom. True or false?
3. What is the name of the mascot of the 1988 Olympic Games?
4. What causes a solar eclipse?
5. Which country owns the Faeroes?
6. What kind of music does Tammy Wynette sing?
7. The largest living thing on earth is nicknamed 'General Sherman'. It measures 24 metres (80 feet) round, and is a good deal taller. What is it?
8. What does Simon Rattle do?
9. Who sailed in the *Santa Maria,* the *Nina* and the *Pinta* in the fifteenth century?
10. What was the Boston Tea Party?

90

1. Who, on television, says, 'I've started so I'll finish'?
2. A clementine is a type of apple. True or false?
3. In which sport might a competitor be penalized for a refusal, or for running out?
4. What does 'hex' mean in computer terminology?
5. What is the world's highest waterfall?

6. Who appeared in the film *Gregory's Girl* and made a record called 'Love Bomb'?
7. What is a puffball?
8. After which famous theatrical knight is part of the National Theatre named?
9. Who is Robert Zimmerman better known as?
10. What, according to Greek legend, was the Minotaur?

91

1. Who, apart from Pinocchio, is the chief character in the film of that name?
2. 'Acute nasopharyngitis' means a cold. True or false?
3. How many players can be on the field at one time in an American football team?
4. What does an anthropologist study?
5. Which country lies between Panama and Nicaragua?
6. Where in Europe was there a pop festival in June 1987?
7. What is a 'primate' in the animal world?
8. Who wrote *The Cherry Orchard, The Seagull* and *The Three Sisters*?
9. Of which union is Arthur Scargill head?
10. How many years of marriage are celebrated by a silver wedding anniversary?

92

1. Who hosts *The Frame Game*?
2. *Cha* is the Chinese word for tea. True or false?
3. What race takes place between Mortlake and Putney in London?
4. What does an oersted measure?
5. Which mountains run along the western side of South America: the Himalayas, the Rockies or the Andes?
6. Who are Clark Datcher, Mike Nocito and Calvin Hays?
7. What do peewits and lapwings have in common?
8. Which French artist of the late nineteenth and early twentieth centuries is famous for his paintings of ballet dancers?
9. What did Roald Amundsen do?
10. In which London square did a nightingale sing, according to the song?

93

1. Who is Donald Duck's girlfriend?
2. The planet Jupiter can be recognized by the rings round it. True or false?

3. Which two countries compete for the Ashes in cricket?
4. Where in England did Marconi receive his historic radio signal from Newfoundland?
5. In which sea is the island of Corsica?
6. Who are the Appleby girls better known as?
7. How many legs has an insect?
8. In which Shakespeare play do witches chant, 'Double, double toil and trouble; Fire burn, and cauldron bubble'?
9. Who was Johann Gutenberg?
10. What was extraordinary about the mythological dog Cerberus?

94

1. In which James Bond film did Oddjob appear?
2. Great Salt Lake is in Morocco. True or false?
3. Where does the Round the Bays Race take place?
4. For what medical discoveries is Louis Pasteur famous?
5. In which European city is the Parthenon?
6. What kind of songs does Tom Paxton sing?
7. What is a lamprey?
8. What was the name of Mr Wackford Squeers's Academy in Charles Dickens's novel *Nicholas Nickleby*?
9. How many times was Winston Churchill prime minister of Britain?
10. Who was Dandini?

95

1. Who was the manager of the Sports Centre in *Crossroads*?
2. The Goliath frog of West Africa is nearly a metre in length. True or false?
3. Who wears the *maillot jaune,* or yellow jersey?
4. Which terrible weapon did Julius Robert Oppenheimer design and construct?
5. Where is Dum Dum Airport?
6. The singer of 'Nothing's Gonna Stop Me Now' is better known as – what?
7. What kind of creature is an onager?
8. Which great Russian ballet dancer was famed for his partnership with Margot Fonteyn?
9. What did Sir Rowland Hill do in 1840?
10. How did Noah know when the Flood was receding?

96

1. Who plays Fallon in *The Colbys*?
2. Tallahassee is a town in California, USA. True or false?
3. Which football team is known as the Gulls?
4. What instruments do sailors in submarines use to see above the water when submerged?
5. Where is the Barents Sea?
6. Who had a 'Big Love'?
7. Can penguins fly?

8. What is RADA?
9. Who, according to tradition, was forced to shoot an apple off his son's head?
10. What notable event in British history took place on 12 May 1937?

97

1. His *Coronation Street* wife was called Gail. Who is he?
2. £50 bank notes include a laser-engraved pattern to prevent forgery. True or false?
3. Which famous black athlete swept the board at the 1936 Olympics?
4. Where in the body would you find the cerebrum?
5. What is the remotest inhabited island in the world?
6. How many men/women are there in Swing Out Sister?
7. What are Ayrshires, Friesians and Jerseys?
8. Who was Molière?
9. One brother is a famous actor and film director; the other is a distinguished naturalist and TV personality. Who are they?
10. Who was England's common enemy at both Trafalgar and Waterloo?

98

1. What was *Star Trek IV* called?
2. People could be hanged for cutting down trees in Britain until 1819. True or false?
3. With which sport is the Royal and Ancient ____ Club of St Andrews associated?
4. What, in chemistry, is a suspension?
5. What is the largest inland sea in the world?
6. Who are the four members of Curiosity Killed the Cat?
7. What do the sundew, the pitcher plant and the Venus fly trap have in common?
8. Who was Nijinsky?
9. Who succeeded George IV to the English throne?
10. What happened in Dallas, Texas, in November 1963 to change the fate of a nation?

99

1. Who hosts *Countdown*?
2. A pyracantha is a type of South American snake. True or false?
3. Which sportsmen might 'feather' something?
4. What is a joystick used for on a computer?
5. What was the Sellafield nuclear reprocessing plant formerly called?
6. Who sang 'Time Will Crawl'?
7. Which creature spends its life travelling

from the Sargasso Sea in the Atlantic Ocean to Europe's rivers and back again?

8. Who said, 'Once more unto the breach, dear friends, once more . . .' according to Shakespeare?
9. Who was Henry VIII's Chancellor?
10. What is a soufflé?

100/6   The Singing World

100

1. Who played the Irish R.M. on television?
2. After the 1987 General Election Sir Geoffrey Howe became Home Secretary. True or false?
3. In which sport might you use a half nelson?
4. What does a geophysicist do?
5. On which of America's Great Lakes is Chicago?
6. 'I'd Like to Teach the World to Sing' was adapted from a Coca Cola advert. Who made it a hit?
7. What kind of creature is a sidewinder?
8. What do two violins, a viola and a cello make?
9. Who was Lord Darnley's wife?
10. What do the initials F. R. C. V. S. stand for?

101

1. In which recent film did Harrison Ford play an inventor in the jungles of Central America?
2. Arabic is written from left to right. True or false?
3. Which is the odd man out: Derby, Grand National, St Leger?
4. Which famous computer generates random numbers enabling people to win large sums of money?
5. What is the name of the large red rock formation in central Australia?
6. Which group did Johnny Rotten and Sid Vicious belong to?
7. What kind of fruits are oranges, lemons, grapefruits and limes?
8. What does the German word *lieder* mean in musical terms?
9. Which princes was Richard III alleged to have murdered in the Tower of London?
10. Which reference book is known as the O. E. D.?

102

1. What kind of TV show does Joan Rivers host?
2. Part of Mont Blanc is in Italy, and part in France. True or false?
3. What was Nadia Comaneci's sport?
4. What do the letters in the word 'laser' stand for?

5. Which river flows through Rome?
6. What, in the children's song, did the bells of St Clement's sing?
7. What are williams, conference and comice?
8. What was Philip Marlowe's job in the exciting stories by Raymond Chandler?
9. For what is Bram Stoker famous?
10. Which boy soprano sang the theme music from *The Snowman*, 'Walking on the Air'?

103

1. Who presents the Video Report on *Good Morning, Britain*?
2. Alexander Pope was a famous scientist. True or false?
3. What happens at Brands Hatch, Silverstone and Oulton Park?
4. What is the total length of blood vessels in the human body? Is it approximately 1000 kilometres (620 miles), 1500 kilometres (930 miles) or 2500 kilometres (1560 miles)?
5. Where and what is Alcatraz?
6. Who sang, 'I Wanna Dance with Somebody Who Loves Me'?
7. Which fish is born in fresh water, moves to the sea to feed and grow, and returns to the river where it was hatched to breed?
8. With which form of the arts is Anthony Dowell associated?
9. What did Frank Winfield Woolworth found?
10. Who in Britain is allowed to own cars without number plates?

104

1. What's the name of Deirdre Barlow's daughter in *Coronation Street*?
2. Richmal Crompton was a famous painter. True or false?
3. In which year was the Fastnet Race disaster: 1978, 1979 or 1980?
4. What is Braille?
5. What was the city of Leningrad formerly called?
6. To which famous rock and roll star was the actress who plays *Dynasty*'s Jenna Wade married?
7. What is unusual about the place in which a skylark builds its nest?
8. Who is Alice Marks better known as in the ballet world?
9. Whose hiding in an oak tree led to the celebration of 29 May as Oak Apple Day?
10. What kind of flower might be a 'hybrid tea'?

105

1. What's the name of the rabbit in *Bambi*?
2. St George's Day is 21 April. True or false?

3. Which rider holds the British high jump record in show jumping: is it Michael Whitaker, Harvey Smith or Nick Skelton?
4. What is an electrolyte?
5. Near which capital city is Dun Laoghaire?
6. By what name is Annie Mae Bullock better known?
7. Which large bird of the crow family is black and white?
8. Who were Elgar and Delius?
9. What was thriller writer Dick Francis's former profession?
10. What are hieroglyphics?

106

1. Where were the characters based in *Auf Wiedersehen, Pet*?
2. Damascus has been inhabited since 2000 BC. True or false?
3. What is unusual about baseball players' socks?
4. Of which element is Pb the symbol?
5. Which river flows through Paris?
6. Who wrote and sang the song about Marilyn Monroe, 'Candle in the Wind'?
7. Of which creatures is herpetology a study?
8. What does Dietrich Fischer-Dieskau do?
9. Who are the two famous sisters who both have the same initials, one of whom is an actress and one of whom is a writer?
10. Who was called 'the fat owl of the Remove'?

107

1. What is the name of the starship commanded by Captain Kirk?
2. Mousehole is a town in Cornwall. True or false?
3. Who won the men's singles title in the 1987 Wimbledon tennis championships?
4. For what is Samuel Finley Breese Morse famous?
5. Which city of south-west England is known for its elegant Georgian buildings and thermal springs?
6. Who was George Michael's partner in the Wham! duo?
7. Do snakes hibernate?
8. In which Shakespeare play do the Capulets and the Montagues appear?
9. Who was 'Capability' Brown?
10. Who is the Lord Chancellor of Britain?

108

1. What kind of animal is Roland Rat's friend Errol?
2. Skoda cars are made in Spain. True or false?
3. Which great athlete was defeated in Madrid in June 1986 after an unbeaten run of nine years, nine months and nine days?
4. What is a floppy disc?
5. Where, in the USA, is the Pentagon?
6. How is Marvin Lee Aday beter known?

7. What kind of animal is a gecko?
8. Who wrote a poem about Miss Joan Hunter Dunn?
9. How did John Wilkes Booth become famous?
10. What is notable about the numbers 53, 89 and 109?

flip flop

108/4   An unsuccessful record?

109

1. Whose catchphrase is 'Boom, boom!'?
2. Salvador Dali was a famous cellist. True or false?
3. Who would use a piton?
4. What does claustrophobia mean?
5. In which country in the southern hemisphere is Table Mountain?
6. Who 'Can't Be With You Tonight'?
7. What is meant by pollarding a tree?
8. Who wrote *Arms and the Man*, *Man and Superman* and *Saint Joan*?
9. Which famous dancing star died in June 1987?
10. Which Western movie star was elected mayor of a California town?

110

1. Who are the presenters of *The Animals Roadshow*?
2. Irving Berlin was a famous composer. True or false?
3. In the Isle of Man TT races, what does TT stand for?
4. What is the speed of sound?
5. Which two countries does Offa's Dyke separate?
6. What was Elvis Presley's nickname?
7. What are pointers, setters and retrievers?
8. What was Shylock's nationality?
9. Whom did Wallis Warfield Simpson marry in 1937?
10. Which Sunday newspaper produces *YOU* magazine?

welcome to The Animals Road show!

110/1   ??????

111

1. Who is the latest film James Bond?
2. Alexis Carrington is a character in *Dallas*. True or false?

3. How many players are there in a polo team?
4. Which is the odd man out: argon, silicon, xenon?
5. What is the capital of Finland?
6. Who, in a classic sixties' hit, was a 'little red rooster'?
7. Which is the largest land-living, meat-eating animal on earth: the lion, the polar bear, or the kodiak bear of Alaska?
8. Who, according to Shakespeare, said, 'A horse, a horse, my kingdom for a horse'?
9. With which religion was Brigham Young associated?
10. What takes place at the Snape Maltings, near Aldeburgh in Suffolk?

112

1. Who works with the puppet Sooty?
2. Gouache is a kind of peppery stew. True or false?
3. What game do the Philadelphia Eagles play?
4. For what is Igor Sikorsky famous?
5. What and where is Cotopaxi?
6. Who sang 'Hold Me Now'?
7. In what type of terrain might you hear a curlew?
8. Who was Donatello?
9. Which member of the Royal Family was born on 21 April 1926 at Bruton Street in London's West End?
10. What does H.M.S.O. stand for?

113

1. Who was D.A.R.Y.L., in the film of that name?
2. The Sahara Desert is as large as America. True or false?
3. How far apart are the wickets on a cricket pitch?
4. What is quicksilver another name for?
5. Which is further east, Brighton or Eastbourne?
6. From which hit musical did the song 'Memory' come?
7. What is a Falabella?
8. For what was Sir Thomas Rowlandson known?
9. Which English king signed the Magna Carta?
10. What does N.A.S.A. stand for?

114

1. Who or what was Genevieve in the old film and book?
2. The correct name for a group of crows is a 'murder'. True or false?
3. Which English playground game is the forerunner of baseball?
4. In which direction does a suspended magnet always face?
5. In which English county is Fakenham?
6. Who had a hit with 'Lady in Red'?

7. What is the circumference of the earth at the Equator? Is it approximately 40,000 kilometres (25,000 miles), 50,000 kilometres (31,000 miles) or 25,000 kilometres (15,500 miles)?
8. In which Shakespeare play did Caliban appear?
9. What was Elizabeth Fry known for?
10. Whose horse was Marengo?

115

1. Whose human is Keith Harris?
2. The feast day of St Swithin is 15 August. True or false?
3. In which sport was Stanley Matthews famous?
4. For which element is Zn the symbol?
5. In which Spanish city is the Alhambra?
6. Whose hit album was 'Can't Slow Down'?
7. Where would you find algae?
8. Whose poem about a skylark began 'Hail to thee, blithe spirit'?
9. Who is said to have discovered a scientific principle in his bath, causing him to leap out of it shouting 'Eureka!'?
10. What might have a R.A.M.?

116

1. Which famous film was about the Von Trapp family in Austria?
2. 'Occident' is the opposite of 'orient'. True or false?
3. In which sport would a player use a 'penholder' grip?
4. In which fresh foods is vitamin C found?
5. In which English county is Fowey?
6. Who might be Aladdin Sane?
7. In which continent is the coldest place in the world?
8. Which famous painting is known as 'La Gioconda'?
9. What was Ronald Reagan's profession before he became a politician?
10. In which country would you see an autobahn?

117

1. What TV programme does Frank Bough present?
2. On 25 January the Scots celebrate the birthday of Robert Burns with haggis suppers. True or false?
3. In which sport might someone be a 'dan'?
4. What is the American space programme called Apollo concerned with?
5. In which European city is the famous Little Mermaid statue?

6. Which folk singer had a hit with the hymn 'All Things Bright and Beautiful'?
7. What is a raptor?
8. In which Dickens' novel did Scrooge appear?
9. Which child film star of the 1940s became an American ambassador?
10. Which is the oldest university in Britain?

116/7   The coldest place in the World?

118

1. Who plays J. R. in *Dallas*?
2. Dan Maskell is a famous cricket commentator. True or false?
3. What kind of sportsman might do a Lutz or a Salchow?
4. What is a lodestone?
5. What is the biggest city in Africa?
6. Which jazz singer was the film *Lady Sings the Blues* about?
7. Which creatures do ants 'milk'?
8. Who wrote *Jane Eyre*?
9. What is Bruce Oldfield's profession?
10. Which was the first National Park in Great Britain?

119

1. Which gangster film was entirely acted by children?
2. Translated into English, the name of Giuseppe Verdi, the great operatic composer, means 'Joe Green'. True or false?
3. For which English county did Ian Botham play cricket in 1987?
4. What is a catalyst?
5. What is the capital of Northern Ireland?
6. With which kind of pop music are Deep Purple, Led Zeppelin and Status Quo associated?
7. What kind of creature builds a drey?
8. Who wrote *The Water Babies*?
9. Which famous fictional detective did Georges Simenon create?
10. Who was Bilbo Baggins?

120

1. Who starred in *Where Eagles Dare*, *Dirty Harry* and *Every Which Way But Loose*?
2. A giraffe's neck has the same number of bones as a man's. True or false?

3. What score does a bullseye in darts gain?
4. What did Isaac Merrit Singer invent?
5. Which is the second largest city in Britain?
6. 'Message in a Bottle' was the first number one hit – of which group?
7. Which mammals have their own form of radar?
8. What connects Colley Cibber, John Masefield and Cecil Day Lewis?
9. Which members of the Royal Family called their second son Henry Charles Albert David?
10. What is a mazurka?

121

1. What was the name of the 1983 film that started the break-dancing craze?
2. St David's Day is 27 March. True or false?
3. What is Slobodan Zivojinovic's sport?
4. Who formulated the Theory of Relativity?
5. In which modern country is the ancient city of Troy: Turkey, Greece or Iran?
6. Who was 'rockin' round the world' at the Live Aid concert?
7. What is a mallard?
8. Who said, 'Annual income £20, annual expenditure £19. 19s. 6d., result, happiness. Annual income £20, annual expenditure £20. 0s. 6d., result, misery.'?
9. Whose victory at Quebec in 1759 ensured that Canada became a British possession?
10. In which English county is Castle Howard?

122

1. Who was the most famous film Dracula?
2. Tadpoles eat meat. True or false?
3. What, in cricket terms, is a 'yorker'?
4. What did Sir James Dewar invent?
5. In which English county is Daventry?
6. How is Steveland Morris better known?
7. Which of the following animals are rodents: hare, mouse, rabbit, rat?
8. In which form of the arts is Michael Frayn distinguished?
9. What is Alistair Cooke famous for?
10. On which American mountain are the heads of American presidents carved?

123

1. With whom are Gavin Campbell, Doc Cox, Adrian Mills and Grant Baynham regularly seen on television?
2. Aspirin is contained in the bark of willow trees. True or false?
3. If an athlete is competing in a 400-metre race, does he or she have to stay in the same lane for the whole race?
4. In which form of science was Tycho Brahe distinguished?
5. What are the Dodecanese: mountains, islands or marshes?
6. Who had a hit with 'Reet Petite' in 1986?
7. Approximately how many species of

ladybirds are found in Britain: ten, twenty or over forty?

8. Who wrote the opera *Tosca*?
9. Who is Britain's Chancellor of the Exchequer?
10. How many players are there in a game of bridge?

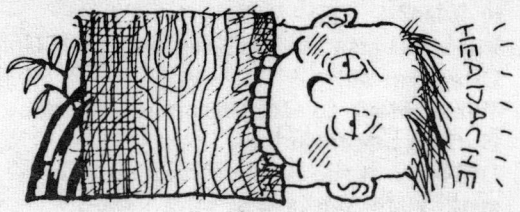

123/2   Aspirin grows on trees?

124

1. Which television programme is introduced by Jonathan King?
2. The General Strike in Britain took place in 1936. True or false?
3. Which football team's home ground is Old Trafford?
4. What is a proton?
5. In which country is the battlefield of Waterloo?
6. Which band does Bono Vox belong to?
7. What does a cormorant eat?
8. In which Dickens novel does Miss Havisham appear?
9. Which royal family did Princess Anastasia belong to?
10. Which lovable children's book character adores marmalade sandwiches?

125

1. Which much-loved cartoon featured the song 'When You Wish Upon a Star'?
2. At a certain point Russia and America are only three kilometres (two miles) apart. True or false?
3. For what sport is the King George V Gold Cup awarded?
4. What colour do sodium compounds colour a Bunsen burner flame?
5. Only one of the Seven Wonders of the World still exists. What is it?
6. The Beatles made a record called 'I Wanna Kiss Your Hand' — or did they?
7. Where do frogs spend the winter?
8. For what form of art was Gustave Doré known?
9. For what is Ernest Henry Shackleton famous?
10. What is a pollack: a fish, a tree, or a musical instrument?

126

1. Who, or what, are Heathcliff and Marmaduke?
2. The longest railway tunnel in Great Britain is the Totley Tunnel near Sheffield. True or false?
3. How did Peter Doohan amaze fans at Wimbledon in 1987?

4. What does a newton measure?
5. In which European city is the Brandenburg Gate?
6. Which legendary singer of hits such as 'Peggy Sue' and 'Maybe Baby' was killed in a plane crash in 1959?
7. What is a female horse under the age of four called?
8. Which instrument does Mstislav Rostropovich play?
9. Who is Ruth Rendell?
10. Which English cathedral has the tallest spire?

127

1. Who was Gary Cooper's female partner in the Western classic *High Noon*?
2. David Bowie has a son called Zowie. True or false?
3. What was Bunny Austin's sport?
4. What function does chlorophyll perform in plants?
5. Which modern city stands where Carthage used to be?
6. Who wrote and recorded 'Blowin' in the Wind' and 'The Times They Are A-Changin''?
7. What types of animal are the Maine Coon, the Birman and the Turkish Van?
8. Which famous Christmas oratorio contains the 'Hallelujah Chorus'?
9. Who is Charles Haughey?
10. When is the Ides of March?

128

1. Who are the three stars of the famous classic film *Some Like It Hot*?
2. *Buona sera* is Spanish for 'Good evening'. True or false?
3. For what did Charlotte Dod become famous in 1887?
4. In which science might you use calculus?
5. Where in Britain is the National Motor Museum?
6. Who topped the hit parade with 'It's A Sin'?
7. Jersey Royals, Maris Piper and King Edward VII are all types of – what?
8. Who wrote the poem 'The Lady of Shalott'?
9. Who was Rob Roy?
10. What will happen to Hong Kong in 1997?

129/7   A toothless tortoise?

129

1. Which famous father and daughter starred in the seventies' film *Paper Moon*?

2. A dead nettle does not sting. True or false?
3. What is Pat Eddery's sport?
4. With which form of matter is Boyle's Law concerned?
5. What have Pompeii and Herculaneum in common?
6. Which Beatles' song began 'Picture yourself in a boat on a river, with tangerine trees and marmalade skies'?
7. Do turtles and tortoises have teeth?
8. Who wrote the opera *La Traviata*?
9. What was Amy Johnson's great achievement?
10. What is ratatouille?

130

1. In what TV police series did David Soul star?
2. Mike Hailwood was a famous footballer. True or false?
3. What was Pat Smythe's sport?
4. Which is the largest castle in England?
5. What has Saltash in common with Plymouth?
6. How is Richard Starkey better known?
7. What's the difference between a monkey and an ape?
8. Who wrote the poem that begins, 'Season of mists and mellow fruitfulness'?
9. What political office does Jacques Chirac hold in France?
10. What is the London street Hatton Garden famous for?

131

1. What was the name of the hippie in *The Young Ones*?
2. Steven Spielberg is an American actor. True or false?
3. Who won the 1987 women's singles title in the French tennis championships, to become the youngest holder of the title?
4. How long does a spacecraft take to travel to Mars? Is it approximately three months, seven months or eleven months?
5. What is the capital of Switzerland?
6. Who was 'Under the Boardwalk' in 1987?
7. How can naturalists tell the age of a fish?
8. In which form of the arts was Henri de Toulouse-Lautrec distinguished?
9. Who invented the spinning machine called the mule?
10. Which substance is put in some water supplies to try to prevent tooth decay?

132

1. 'Herbie' appeared in *The Love Bug* and *Herbie Rides Again*. Who or what was Herbie?
2. The smallest lizard in the world is only two centimetres (¾ inch) long. True or false?
3. Which boxer was known as the 'Brown Bomber'?

4. What is the difference between a burette and a pipette?
5. In which European capital is the Rijksmuseum?
6. Which number nervous breakdown did the Rolling Stones have in their sixties' hit?
7. Name three mammals who spend all their lives in water?
8. What is the title of this Shakespeare play: *Timon of* _____ ?
9. What is Henri 'Douanier' Rousseau famous for?
10. With what fictional character do you associate the writer Alf Prøysen ?

131/7   Well it says so here, so it must be true.

THE ANSWERS

1

1. *Jaws.*
2. False, it is a lawyer.
3. At Epsom in Surrey.
4. The study of plants.
5. New York.
6. Duran Duran's.
7. Eight.
8. Beatrix Potter.
9. Prince Edward.
10. An Eskimo canoe.

2

1. Emmerdale Farm.
2. False, they are in England.
3. John McEnroe.
4. Oxygen.
5. Venice.
6. Nick Kamen.
7. A set.
8. Moscow.
9. George Washington.
10. When crossing a road, it is a guide to pedestrians on road safety.

3

1. Tommy Cannon.
2. True.
3. Football.
4. Blue.
5. Sheffield.
6. Frankie Goes to Hollywood.
7. The oak.

8. *Robinson Crusoe*.
9. Tommy Cooper.
10. A hectare.

4

1. Michael J. Fox.
2. False, it is part of Los Angeles.
3. Baseball.
4. Weather forecasting – it measures atmospheric pressure.
5. The Thames.
6. Mike Smith.
7. Red, orange, yellow, green, blue, indigo, violet.
8. The violin.
9. None.
10. In the Tower of London.

5

1. Charlie Chaplin.
2. True.
3. Swansea City.
4. It was the name of the first U.S. space shuttle.
5. Holland.
6. Country music.
7. Doves and pigeons.
8. It is a famous opera house.
9. They were the first men to climb Mount Everest.
10. Pounds, shillings and pence.

6

1. 101.
2. True.
3. Seoul, Korea.
4. Thirty-two.
5. Wellington.
6. Fun, love and money.
7. A kind of terrier.
8. Five.
9. A former president of France.
10. A bell.

7

1. SuperTed.
2. False – it used to be called Ceylon.
3. Zola Budd.
4. A computer.
5. Off the coast of the Isle of Wight.
6. AꓭBA
7. Through its gills.
8. Juliet.
9. The broadcaster Richard Dimbleby.
10. James Callaghan.

8

1. The Queen Vic.
2. False, it is frozen vapour. Hail is frozen rain.
3. The achievement of a bowler who dismisses three batsmen with three consecutive balls.
4. In the mouth – they are teeth.
5. Paris.
6. Shakin' Stevens.
7. Antarctica.
8. Alice, in *Alice in Wonderland*.
9. An American gangster.
10. Greece.

9

1. Foretells the future; he is an astrologer.
2. True.
3. Golf.
4. Attract each other.
5. Florence.
6. The Beastie Boys.
7. Butterflies.
8. Handel.
9. Alexander Graham Bell.
10. 1977.

10

1. The writer and zoo-owner Gerald Durrell.
2. True.

3. A sailing dinghy.
4. 100°C, 212°F.
5. Belgium.
6. Richmond.
7. A Manx.
8. The Three Musketeers.
9. The Sundance Kid.
10. Green.

11

1. *The Hitch-Hiker's Guide to the Galaxy.*
2. True.
3. Motor racing.
4. He invented waterproof cloth.
5. France and Spain.
6. Bob Marley.
7. Rabbits.
8. At the Albert Hall in London.
9. She was burnt at the stake.
10. London and Edinburgh.

12

1. Mondays, Wednesdays and Fridays.
2. False, it is used to measure wind speed.
3. The English Channel.
4. Common salt.
5. In Paris.
6. Police.
7. Swallow.
8. Enid Blyton.
9. King Arthur's.
10. Aer Lingus.

13

1. A ship.
2. False, it is a fruit.
3. A New Zealand rugby team.
4. James Watt.
5. Mecca.
6. *Stand By Me.*

7. An animal that can live on land or in water, like a frog.
8. Oliver Twist.
9. Richard Branson.
10. Seventy miles per hour (112 kilometres per hour).

14

1. Clark Kent.
2. True.
3. Snooker, billiards and pool.
4. An astronomer.
5. North America and Asia.
6. Madonna.
7. A house plant.
8. Winnie the Pooh's.
9. Publishing newspapers.
10. A ship.

15

1. Gave the weather forecast.
2. False, it is a dance.
3. The Marylebone Cricket Club.
4. Sulphuric acid.
5. The Zambesi.
6. Elton John.
7. In a flower.
8. Soprano.
9. Japan.
10. Railway systems of, respectively, America, Britain and France.

16

1. Sean Connery.
2. True.
3. Show jumping.
4. The joints.
5. Australia.
6. UB40's.
7. The ostrich.
8. *Cinderella.*

9. St Francis of Assissi.
10. A kind of pasta.

17

1. By helicopter.
2. False, Charles Dickens wrote it.
3. A judo expert.
4. A mammal.
5. Havana.
6. Doves.
7. In the spring.
8. Six.
9. King John.
10. Her Majesty Queen Elizabeth the Queen Mother.

18

1. Patrick Troughton.
2. True.
3. Fifteen.
4. He became the first man in space.
5. Paris.
6. Jon Moss.
7. The fruits of the rose and the hawthorn.
8. Loud.
9. Jacob's.
10. Highgrove House.

19

1. Indiana Jones.
2. False. Like all animals, they drink water.
3. Twenty-six miles 385 yards (42.195 kilometres).
4. Iron.
5. In Wales.
6. Sigue Sigue Sputnik.
7. A breed of heavy horse.
8. A kind of print.
9. Henry Morton Stanley, the British explorer and journalist.
10. A water spout in the shape of a grotesque figure or face which projects from the gutter of a building.

20 _____

1. Eamonn Andrews.
2. True.
3. Twelve.
4. Blue.
5. The Tropic of Capricorn.
6. Bruce Springsteen.
7. A band of stars in the sky.
8. A famous Australian soprano.
9. George Stephenson.
10. Forty.

21 _____

1. Peter Sellers.
2. True.
3. Sheffield United.
4. Vinegar.
5. The Isles of Scilly.
6. 'Thriller'.
7. Its ability to change the colour of its skin to match its surroundings.
8. Leonardo da Vinci.
9. King Canute.
10. 'Ladies' and 'gentlemen'.

22 _____

1. *The Guinness Book of Records.*
2. False, it is on the Firth of Forth.
3. Coventry City.
4. Every seventy-five or seventy-six years.
5. In the centre of Australia.
6. Maud.
7. The yellowhammer's.
8. Bertie Wooster's, in the novels by P. G. Wodehouse.
9. Napoleon.
10. A French fish soup.

23 _____

1. Paul Hogan.
2. False, it is a breed of dog.

3. Fourteen.
4. Approximately 1500 mph (2414 km/h).
5. Dublin.
6. *Cats,* based on *Old Possum's Book of Practical Cats.*
7. None.
8. Van Gogh's.
9. Italian.
10. Types of china.

24

1. Christine (Cagney) and Mary Beth (Lacey).
2. True.
3. Every four years.
4. A digital computer.
5. On Salisbury Plain in Wiltshire, England.
6. Sergeant Pepper.
7. A horse chestnut.
8. Fourteen.
9. Princess Margaret.
10. Paper.

25

1. BBC 1.
2. True.
3. Shoot them, they are targets.
4. No, it is Herstmonceux Castle in East Sussex.
5. Warsaw.
6. They are both DJs.
7. A flower.
8. The Brontës.
9. President Kennedy.
10. A Spanish scarf, worn by women over the head and shoulders.

26

1. They all starred Paul Newman.
2. True.
3. Riding, fencing, swimming, shooting and running.
4. Neil Armstrong.
5. Harley Street.

6. Nick Berry (Wicksy).
7. A young hare.
8. Picasso, he was a painter. The others were composers.
9. He was the architect who designed it.
10. A vegetable, a type of small marrow.

27

1. Whales.
2. False, he had six.
3. Tennis.
4. Computer languages.
5. In Birmingham.
6. Michael Jackson's.
7. The pearl.
8. Sherlock Holmes's.
9. An epic poet of ancient Greece.
10. The *Marseillaise*.

28

1. The Marx Brothers.
2. False, it is Canberra.
3. Cricket.
4. Metallic objects containing iron.
5. In Westminster Abbey.
6. Boy George.
7. Bright blue.
8. Macbeth.
9. The Pope.
10. Its theatres.

29

1. Grange Hill.
2. False, it was a man's tight-fitting jacket.
3. Leeds United.
4. Blue.
5. Paris.
6. Barry Manilow's.
7. An ewe.
8. Anne, in the novel by L. M. Montgomery.

9. A former Conservative MP and author.
10. ¾.

30

1. *Santa Claus.*
2. False, they collect nectar with which to make honey.
3. Long-distance walking.
4. Mercury, it is a liquid metal. The others are solid metals.
5. Wall Street.
6. Bob Geldof's.
7. Brown.
8. Dvorak.
9. Belgium.
10. Maize.

31

1. Dennis Waterman.
2. True.
3. Alain Prost.
4. Sound.
5. The Chancellor of the Exchequer.
6. Australia.
7. No, it is a mammal.
8. He was a famous Italian Renaissance sculptor, architect and painter. Probably his best-known works are his statue of David, and the paintings on the ceiling of the Sistine Chapel in Rome.
9. King Wenceslas.
10. Saturday.

32

1. *Emerald.*
2. True.
3. Ice hockey.
4. In citrus fruits such as oranges, lemons and grapefruit.
5. Pisa.
6. Chris de Burgh.
7. The colorado beetle.
8. A Dutch abstract painter who concentrated on geometrical shapes.
9. China.
10. 1 November.

33

1. Gian Sammarco.
2. False, she is MP for Finchley.
3. Cricket.
4. A stand for supporting instruments.
5. San Francisco.
6. Ultravox.
7. To catch insects for food.
8. Trumpet — it is a brass instrument. All the rest are woodwind instruments.
9. The revolver.
10. 1982.

34

1. Dangermouse.
2. True.
3. Muhammad Ali.
4. 0 and 1.
5. East Germany.
6. Billy Idol.
7. The cheetah, at 96–101 kilometres per hour (60–63 miles per hour).
8. Sculpture.
9. Mime.
10. A game.

35 _____

1. He is a Detective Chief Inspector.
2. True.
3. Amateur Athletics Association.
4. Hydrogen sulphide.
5. Edinburgh.
6. Echo and the Bunnymen.
7. It is a breed of African dog which does not bark.
8. Beethoven.
9. The police force (in London in 1829).
10. An international news agency.

36 _____

1. *Monty Python's Flying Circus*.
2. False, there is no such animal.
3. A bobsleigh run at St Moritz in Switzerland.
4. 1200 km/h (750 mph).
5. Over the River Humber.
6. Buck's Fizz.
7. A young swan.
8. *The Nutcracker*.
9. Georg and Laszlo Biro.
10. A beagle.

37 _____

1. Chris Serle and Paul Heiney.
2. True.
3. Basketball.
4. Gold.
5. The Pacific.
6. Shalamar.
7. Africa, south-east Asia and South America.
8. Painting, especially portrait painting.
9. George IV.
10. A Japanese woman.

38

1. *Third.*
2. True.
3. Card games.
4. X-rays.
5. Sydney, Australia.
6. Madness.
7. The sturgeon.
8. The English National Opera.
9. The computer.
10. Oats.

39

1. Supergran's.
2. True.
3. Reference Point, ridden by Steve Cauthen.
4. The bouncing bomb.
5. The Midlands area around Birmingham.
6. Soul and gospel music.
7. A legless lizard.
8. Lah.
9. Television.
10. An island.

40

1. Jools Holland.
2. True.
3. Everton.
4. Mathematics.
5. In the north of Northern Ireland, in what was Country Antrim.
6. Simon Le Bon.
7. Rabbits.
8. A Russian ballerina.
9. Henry V.
10. Admiral Nelson.

41

1. A TV weatherman.
2. True.

3. Eleven.
4. André Marie Ampère.
5. In the Outer Hebrides. They are islands.
6. Cliff Richard.
7. Willows.
8. Bizet, he was a composer. The others were artists.
9. Lady Godiva.
10. The Royal National Lifeboat Institution.

42

1. *All Creatures Great and Small.*
2. False, he was a famous French writer.
3. Curling.
4. Sir Alexander Fleming.
5. A tomb.
6. America, in their 1987 hit.
7. Dutch elm disease.
8. A ballet dancer.
9. Richard III.
10. A bicycle.

43

1. Sue Cook and Nick Ross.
2. False, it is a kind of tree.
3. Fatima Whitbread.
4. The lungs.
5. Scafell.
6. UB40.
7. A swan. A cob is a male swan, a pen a female.
8. Andrés Segovia.
9. The British Queen of the Iceni in the first century AD.
10. At sea — it means seasickness.

44

1. *The Empire Strikes Back.*
2. True.
3. A cross-country horse race over fences, organized by a hunt.
4. A negatively-charged particle of an atom.
5. Rio de Janeiro, Brazil.
6. A farm.
7. Australia.
8. *Peter Pan.*
9. Thomas à Becket.
10. A horse.

45

1. *Blockbusters.*
2. True.
3. Squash.
4. One that is easy to use and understand.
5. In the North Sea.
6. Annie Lennox.
7. Types of duck.
8. Roald Dahl.
9. Michael Foot.
10. A steam locomotive.

46

1. Ethel.
2. False, it is a tall blue flower.
3. In August.
4. It is a natural force that attracts bodies towards the earth.
5. In Wyoming, USA.
6. Detroit.
7. An animal that carries its young in a pouch.
8. Writing limericks and nonsense poems.
9. Lot's.
10. In America, it would be a bus.

47

1. Jerry.
2. True.
3. Football.
4. Rudolph Diesel.
5. Mustard.
6. Andy, John and Roger.
7. Barbary apes.
8. HMS *Pinafore*.
9. King Alfred.
10. Bicycle motor cross.

48

1. Eddie Murphy.
2. False, it is a kind of monkey.
3. Boxing.
4. 1976.
5. The islands which make up Japan.
6. The trumpet.
7. Five.
8. Raymond Briggs.
9. Queen Elizabeth I's.
10. Italy and France.

49

1. *Carry on Cleo*.
2. True.
3. Dennis Taylor.
4. A computer.
5. Turkey.
6. Mick Jagger and David Bowie.
7. O.
8. Mozart.
9. The former American president Theodore Roosevelt.
10. In Houston, Texas.

50

1. The doomed planet Krypton.
2. True.
3. A cycle race, also known as the Tour of Britain.

4. Read only memory.
5. Copenhagen.
6. A-Ha.
7. A type of plant that grows on stones and tree trunks.
8. J. S. Bach.
9. Lord Nelson's.
10. The M62.

51

1. *A horse*.
2. False, it was built in the reign of William I.
3. 11.11 centimetres (4 inches).
4. 186,000 miles per second.
5. In the Netherlands.
6. Liverpool.
7. A toadstool.
8. A nineteenth-century English woman novelist.
9. He is a playwright.
10. A pavement.

52

1. Frank Carson's.
2. True.
3. Red Rum.
4. Birds.
5. Venezuela.
6. Marillion.
7. The elephant.
8. *My Fair Lady* is the film/musical of the play *Pygmalion*.
9. Lady Diana Spencer.
10. Red and amber.

53

1. Lizzie Webb.
2. True.
3. The continents of Europe, the Americas, Africa, Australia and Asia.
4. The red colouring matter of the blood.
5. Munich.

6. Pussy.
7. A creature that lives in a shell, like a snail.
8. Redgrave.
9. Sir Robert Walpole.
10. Derbyshire.

54

1. In *That's My Dog*.
2. False, they are types of apple.
3. Jackie Stewart.
4. Carbon dioxide.
5. Dorset.
6. Wham!
7. A type of freshwater fish.
8. Wagner.
9. Mark Thatcher.
10. *R*adio *d*etection *a*nd *r*anging.

55

1. The A-Team.
2. True.
3. Swimming.
4. About the size of your fist.
5. Australia.
6. As Limahl.
7. An aromatic herb.
8. Ted Hughes.
9. 1605.
10. Eat it, it is a kind of bread.

56

1. Stephen Boxer.
2. False, they are all female.
3. Golf.
4. 0°C, 32°F.
5. In Sicily.
6. Bananarama.
7. Cobra, it is the only venomous snake in the list.
8. *Hamlet.*
9. Australia.
10. Dark blue/violet.

57

1. Bernie Clifton.
2. True.
3. Bowling an over in which no runs are scored.
4. The skin.
5. Iraq.
6. The K.B.E.
7. The red deer.
8. Baroness Orczy.
9. Crime. They were two notorious criminals who in the early nineteenth century murdered people and sold their bodies to hospitals for research.
10. Italy.

58

1. Max Headroom.
2. False, it transmits the power from the engine to turn the wheels.
3. Cricket.
4. The circulation of the blood.
5. New York.
6. Paul McCartney.
7. The goldfish.
8. The queen of the fairies, in Shakespeare's *A Midsummer Night's Dream*.
9. Florence Nightingale.
10. David.

59

1. M.
2. True.
3. Hawaii.
4. Christopher Cockerell.
5. Corsica.
6. The Smiths.
7. Between April and September, when the food could be harmful to young birds.
8. Dylan Thomas.
9. The leader of the mutiny on Captain Bligh's ship *Bounty*.
10. 1415.

60

1. Lord Peter Wimsey.
2. True.
3. Steve Davis.
4. Speed and travel time in a motor vehicle.
5. Antarctica.
6. *Chess.*
7. The stoat.
8. *The Mousetrap* by Agatha Christie.
9. Prince Charles.
10. Milk.

61

1. A motel.
2. False, it is a large freshwater fish.
3. Mike Gatting.
4. The spine.
5. Wales and Ireland.
6. The sparrow.
7. Yew trees.
8. *David Copperfield.*
9. From 20 January 1936 to 11 December 1936, though he was never crowned.
10. An Italian car.

62

1. St Trinian's.
2. True.
3. A golf player.
4. Kennedy.
5. Off the south-east coast of Africa.
6. Prince.
7. Volcanoes.
8. His paintings of horses and other animals.
9. A Roman poet.
10. The Bank of England.

63 _____

1. *Seven*.
2. False, it is off the west coast of Scotland.
3. Motor racing.
4. 2.
5. In Morocco.
6. David 'Kid' Jensen.
7. The Pacific.
8. Frances Hodgson Burnett.
9. The Duchess of York.
10. Judas Iscariot.

64 _____

1. Leslie Crowther.
2. False, he was a famous First World War flying ace.
3. A ball and a curved stick like a hockey stick.
4. 1969.
5. In Hyde Park, at Marble Arch in London.
6. Paul Simon.
7. The male.
8. Percussion instruments.
9. The 'Alice' of *Alice in Wonderland*.
10. A metre.

65 _____

1. *Hi-De-Hi*.
2. True.
3. The Royal Regatta – a rowing event.
4. The Great Western Railway.
5. Guernsey's.
6. As Elton John.
7. Earthquakes.
8. The theatre – she was an actress.
9. Benjamin Franklin.
10. Cushion and fashion.

66

1. Jim Davidson.
2. True, it is supposed to have contained arsenic.
3. They are the only British skaters to have won the World, Olympic and European skating titles in the same year (1976 and 1984 respectively).
4. Russian — her name was Valentina Tereshkova.
5. In Paris.
6. Julio Iglesias.
7. A bat.
8. A rest room for the actors.
9. Patrick Moore.
10. Eight.

67

1. *Back to the Future.*
2. True.
3. A rodeo held in Alberta, Canada.
4. BASIC.
5. New Guinea.
6. 'Travel'.
7. Soil below ground level which remains frozen all year round.
8. In Regent's Park.
9. Tatum O'Neal.
10. Bees.

68

1. Barry, Karen, Damon and Claire.
2. True.
3. Twenty-one, unless both players reach twenty in which case the winner is the first to gain a two-point lead.
4. Copper.
5. St Paul's.
6. 'Heartbreak Hotel'.
7. The albatross.
8. He creates ballets and other dance routines.
9. John Buchan.
10. Cambridge.

69 _____

1. *Murphy's Mob.*
2. False, he was a great Italian singer.
3. Indianapolis.
4. A kind of three-dimensional photograph made with a laser.
5. The Appalachians.
6. Rod Stewart's.
7. Tiny sea creatures eaten by whales, seals and birds.
8. A Welsh festival of music and poetry.
9. Chess.
10. Princess Anne's.

70 _____

1. *Susan;* Madonna.
2. True.
3. A mountaineer.
4. Brass, it is an alloy, the others are elements.
5. Iran and the USSR.
6. Frankie Goes to Hollywood.
7. Flowering shrubs.
8. Oscar Wilde.
9. Henry VIII's and Anne Boleyn's.
10. Manchester.

71 _____

1. Three.
2. True.
3. Canoeing, skiing and skateboarding.
4. It bends, or 'refracts' light beams.
5. Somerset.
6. David Bowie.
7. Eat it, it is a kind of fruit.
8. Tchaikovsky.
9. An American president (1933–45).
10. Roman roads.

72 _____

1. Russ Abbott.
2. False.

3. A boundary six.
4. The moon.
5. Florida.
6. The Jackson Five.
7. Types of grass.
8. The Royal Opera House, Covent Garden.
9. Antiques.
10. Red, white and blue.

73

1. The Lone Ranger's Indian friend.
2. True.
3. Seven.
4. It is considered by scientists to be absolute zero.
5. England and Scotland.
6. Elton John.
7. The eagle.
8. It is the appearance distant objects have of being smaller than nearer objects.
9. William IV.
10. At Bladon in Oxfordshire.

74

1. E. T.
2. False. Baking powder or self-raising flour helps them to rise.
3. Dressage.
4. The part just above the inner cone of flame.
5. Lake Ontario.
6. Philadelphia.
7. The snapdragon.
8. The actors' union.
9. He was an American composer of popular music.
10. A tribe of North American Indians.

75 _____

1. The Rover's Return.
2. True.
3. A style of high jumping.
4. German measles.
5. In Portugal.
6. She sang as part of Yazoo before going solo.
7. South America.
8. Schubert.
9. The French Revolution.
10. In its place.

76 _____

1. In Transylvania.
2. True.
3. At Aintree near Liverpool.
4. The chemistry of hydrocarbons and their derivatives.
5. Amsterdam.
6. Echo and the Bunnymen.
7. An African elephant.
8. Manchester and Sheffield.
9. David Frost's.
10. 4 feet 8½ inches (1.43 metres).

77 _____

1. *Greystoke: the Legend of Tarzan, Lord of the Apes.*
2. True.
3. Between fourteen and sixteen.
4. Sulphur.
5. On the Isle of Wight.
6. Boy George.
7. Stalactites.
8. Maria Callas.
9. David Owen, Shirley Williams, William Rodgers and Roy Jenkins.
10. It was the first plane to fly across the Atlantic.

78

1. *The New Avengers.*
2. False, they are blue flowers found in mountain regions.
3. Daley Thompson.
4. There are 206.
5. Venice.
6. *Beverley Hills Cop.*
7. The cuckoo.
8. Scottish Opera.
9. Catherine of Aragon.
10. The underground railway.

79

1. John Craven.
2. True.
3. Long distance running.
4. Dogs.
5. Glasgow.
6. Siouxie.
7. It has a mark resembling a human skull on its body.
8. William Wordsworth.
9. John Lennon.
10. Records details of its flight.

80

1. It was a ballet.
2. True.
3. 1984.
4. Put the sun, instead of the earth, at the centre of the solar system.
5. The Soar.
6. Tom Jones.
7. A heavy horse.
8. An annual opera festival.
9. Louis XVI.
10. Gas.

81

1. Jimmy of the Krankies.
2. True.
3. He was the only unseeded player ever to win Wimbledon.
4. Euclid.
5. Inverness.
6. Wings.
7. The blue whale.
8. Franz Hals.
9. Astronomer-Royal in the early eighteenth century who predicted the return of the comet named after him after seventy-six years.
10. The *Britannia*.

82

1. Peter Purves.
2. False, it is a dessert made with peaches, raspberry sauce and ice-cream.
3. Bryan Robson.
4. Sir Frank Whittle.
5. Ottawa.
6. Mick Jagger.
7. Under the eaves of buildings.
8. Modern paintings.
9. Princess Anne's and Mark Phillips's.
10. Graham Hill.

83

1. *Rainbow*.
2. False – it is a spider.
3. Billie Jean King.
4. The wavelength of light.
5. Lourdes.
6. Vangelis.
7. Fish.
8. Portrait painting.
9. Richard I.
10. He is blind.

84

1. Bugs Bunny.
2. True.
3. Russian and Bulgarian.
4. Botany: he was a Swedish botanist who devised the system of classification for plants and animals.
5. In Paris.
6. Rastafarianism.
7. Blackbirds.
8. Benjamin Britten.
9. William I.
10. Switzerland.

85

1. Pandora.
2. True.
3. Shooting.
4. James Dewar.
5. In New York.
6. Sting.
7. Hares.
8. He murdered her by smothering.
9. Harold Wilson.
10. On an invitation – it means *Répondez, s'il vous plaît* – literally, 'please reply'.

86

1. *Raiders of the Lost Ark.*
2. True.
3. 209 km/h – 130mph.
4. A gland in the body, near the stomach.
5. At Millwall in the River Thames.
6. Frankie Goes to Hollywood.
7. An otter.
8. The words of an opera.
9. Robert the Bruce, fourteenth king of Scotland.
10. A cathedral.

87

1. Barry Humphries.
2. False, it was a Model T Ford car.
3. Ice hockey.
4. Under three hours (two hours 56 minutes 35 seconds on 1 January 1983).
5. Canada — it is their name for a mounted policeman.
6. John Farnham.
7. The stag beetle.
8. *Aida.*
9. Charles I.
10. A polo pony.

88

1. Bernie Winters's.
2. True.
3. Hereford United.
4. Giotto.
5. Birmingham.
6. Donna Allen.
7. It is the most venomous fish in the world.
8. *The Pirates of Penzance.*
9. Pope John Paul II.
10. Berwick Rangers.

89

1. The cartoon mouse hero of Steven Spielberg's film *An American Tail.*
2. True.
3. Hodoni.
4. The passing of the moon between the earth and the sun.
5. Denmark.
6. Country music.
7. A giant sequoia tree in California.
8. He is a conductor.
9. Christopher Columbus.
10. An incident in the American War of Independence in 1773 in which tea was thrown into Boston harbour.

90

1. Magnus Magnusson, in *Mastermind*.
2. False, it is a cross between an orange and a tangerine.
3. Show jumping.
4. Hexadecimal – a system which uses sixteen digits, the numbers 0 to 9 and the letters A to F.
5. Angel Falls in Venezuela.
6. Clare Grogan.
7. A kind of toadstool.
8. Sir Laurence Olivier.
9. Bob Dylan.
10. A monster that was half human, half bull.

91

1. Jiminy Cricket.
2. True.
3. Eleven.
4. People.
5. Costa Rica.
6. Montreux, in Switzerland.
7. A member of the highest order of mammals, which includes man and the great apes.
8. Anton Chekhov.
9. The National Union of Mineworkers.
10. Twenty-five.

92

1. Jimmy Tarbuck.
2. True.
3. The University Boat Race.
4. The strength of a magnetic field.
5. The Andes.
6. Johnny Hates Jazz.
7. They are different names of the same bird.
8. Degas.
9. He was the first man to reach the South Pole (in 1911).
10. Berkeley Square.

93

1. Daisy Duck.
2. False, it is the planet Saturn that has rings round it.
3. England and Australia.
4. Poldhu in Cornwall.
5. The Mediterranean.
6. Mel and Kim.
7. Six.
8. *Macbeth.*
9. A German printer regarded as the inventor of printing from movable type.
10. He had three heads.

94

1. *Goldfinger.*
2. False, it is in America.
3. Auckland, New Zealand.
4. He discovered germs and bacteriology and developed immunization against disease.
5. Athens.
6. Folk songs.
7. A type of jawless fish which resembles an eel.
8. Dotheboys Hall.
9. Twice – 1940–45 and 1951–55.
10. Prince Charming's valet in *Cinderella.*

95

1. Adam Chance.
2. True.
3. The leading rider in the Tour de France cycle race.
4. The atomic bomb.
5. Calcutta.
6. A model, it's Samantha Fox.
7. A wild ass.
8. Rudolf Nureyev.
9. Started the Penny Post.
10. The dove he sent out each day from the Ark returned with an olive leaf in her beak.

96

1. Emma Samms.
2. False, it is a town in Florida, USA.
3. Torquay United.
4. A periscope.
5. North of Finland and the USSR.
6. Fleetwood Mac.
7. No.
8. The Royal Academy of Dramatic Art – where actors and actresses are trained.
9. William Tell.
10. The coronation of King George VI.

97

1. Chris Quinten (Brian Tilsley).
2. True.
3. Jesse Owens.
4. In the head, it is part of the brain.
5. Tristan da Cunha.
6. Two men and one woman.
7. Breeds of dairy cattle.
8. A great French comedy playwright of the seventeenth century.
9. Richard and David Attenborough.
10. Napoleon.

98

1. *The Voyage Home.*
2. True.
3. Golf, which is the missing word.
4. A liquid with solid particles suspended, rather than dissolved, in it.
5. The Caspian Sea.
6. Migi, Ben, Ju and Nick.
7. They are all insect-eating plants.
8. A famous Russian dancer (also a famous English racehorse).
9. William IV.
10. President Kennedy was assassinated.

99

1. Richard Whiteley.
2. False, it is an evergreen flowering shrub.
3. Oarsmen; it is a movement of the oar.
4. To move things around on the screen.
5. Windscale.
6. David Bowie.
7. The common eel.
8. Henry V.
9. Sir Thomas More.
10. A light, frothy baked pudding made with beaten eggs.

100

1. Peter Bowles.
2. False, he was Foreign Secretary.
3. Wrestling.
4. Studies the physics of the earth.
5. Lake Michigan.
6. The New Seekers.
7. A rattlesnake.
8. A string quartet.
9. Mary, Queen of Scots.
10. Fellow of the Royal College of Veterinary Surgeons.

101

1. *The Mosquito Coast.*
2. False, it is written from right to left.
3. Grand National, it is a steeplechase. The others are flat races.
4. Ernie.
5. Ayer's Rock.
6. The Sex Pistols.
7. Citrus fruits.
8. Literally, 'songs'. The singer is often accompanied by a piano.
9. Princes Edward and Richard.
10. The *Oxford English Dictionary.*

102

1. Chat shows.
2. True.
3. Gymnastics.
4. Light *a*mplification by *s*timulated *e*mission of *r*adiation.
5. The Tiber.
6. 'Oranges and lemons'.
7. Types of pear.
8. He was a private detective.
9. He was the author of *Dracula*.
10. Aled Jones.

103

1. Gyles Brandreth.
2. False, he was a famous poet.
3. Motor racing.
4. 2500 kilometres (1560 miles).
5. A former prison on an island in San Francisco Bay, USA.
6. Whitney Houston.
7. The salmon.
8. Ballet.
9. The 'dime store' chain of shops, now Woolworth's.
10. The Queen.

104

1. Tracy.
2. False, she was a famous children's writer.
3. 1979.
4. A system by which blind people can read.
5. St Petersburg.
6. Elvis Presley.
7. It is on the ground.
8. Alicia Markova.
9. Charles II.
10. A rose.

105 _____

1. Thumper.
2. False, it is 23 April.
3. Nick Skelton (7ft 7^5/$_{16}$ in − 2.32 m).
4. A chemical which conducts electricity when dissolved in water.
5. Dublin.
6. Tina Turner.
7. The magpie.
8. British composers.
9. He was a jockey.
10. Figures which stand for words or sounds, as in ancient Egyptian writing.

106 _____

1. West Germany.
2. True.
3. They only go up the outer sides of the legs.
4. Lead.
5. The Seine.
6. Elton John.
7. Reptiles.
8. He is a famous singer.
9. Joan Collins and Jackie Collins.
10. Billy Bunter, in Frank Richards's stories.

107 _____

1. The *Enterprise*.
2. True.
3. Pat Cash.
4. He invented the telegraph and Morse Code.
5. Bath.
6. Andrew Ridgeley.
7. Yes.
8. *Romeo and Juliet*.
9. An eighteenth-century English landscape architect.
10. The Rt. Hon. Lord Mackay of Clashfern.

108
1. A hamster.
2. False, they are made in Czechoslovakia.
3. Edwin Moses.
4. A plastic disc with a magnetically sensitive surface from which a computer picks up information.
5. In Arlington, Virginia.
6. Meat Loaf.
7. A lizard.
8. John Betjeman.
9. He shot President Lincoln.
10. They are prime numbers, which can only be divided evenly by themselves and 1.

109
1. Basil Brush's.
2. False, he was a famous artist.
3. A mountaineer.
4. Fear of enclosed spaces.
5. In South Africa it is near Cape Town.
6. Judy Boucher.
7. Cutting off its branches.
8. George Bernard Shaw.
9. Fred Astaire.
10. Clint Eastwood.

110
1. Sarah Kennedy and Desmond Morris.
2. True.
3. Tourist Trophy.
4. 1225 kilometres per hour (761 miles per hour).
5. England and Wales.
6. Elvis the Pelvis.
7. Gundogs.
8. Jewish.
9. Edward VIII, later the Duke of Windsor.
10. *The Mail on Sunday.*

111

1. Timothy Dalton.
2. False, she is a character in *Dynasty*.
3. Four.
4. Silicon, it is a solid, the others are gases.
5. Helsinki.
6. Mick Jagger.
7. The kodiak bear.
8. Richard III.
9. The Mormon religion.
10. Concerts.

112

1. Matthew Corbett.
2. False, it is a kind of paint.
3. American football.
4. He made the first helicopter.
5. A volcano in Ecuador.
6. Johnny Logan.
7. On open moorland, marshland or fields.
8. An artist and sculptor of fifteenth-century Florence.
9. The Queen.
10. Her Majesty's Stationery Office.

113

1. A Data Analysing Robot Youth Lifeform.
2. True.
3. Twenty metres (22 yards).
4. Mercury.
5. Eastbourne.
6. *Cats*.
7. The smallest breed of horse in the world.
8. He was an eighteenth-century caricaturist.
9. King John.
10. National Aeronautics and Space Administration.

114

1. A veteran car.
2. True.
3. Rounders.

4. North/south.
5. Norfolk.
6. Chris de Burgh.
7. 40,000 kilometres (25,000 miles).
8. *The Tempest.*
9. Her work in improving prison conditions.
10. Napoleon's.

115

1. Orville's.
2. False, it is 15 July.
3. Football.
4. Zinc.
5. Granada.
6. Lionel Richie's.
7. In water, they are tiny plants.
8. Percy Bysshe Shelley's.
9. Archimedes.
10. A computer – it stands for random access memory.

116

1. *The Sound of Music.*
2. True.
3. Table tennis.
4. In fruits, especially oranges, grapefruit, lemons.
5. Cornwall.
6. David Bowie.
7. Antarctica.
8. The Mona Lisa.
9. He was an actor.
10. Germany.

117

1. *Breakfast Time* on BBC 1.
2. True.
3. Judo.
4. Manned exploration of the moon.
5. Copenhagen.
6. Donovan.
7. A bird of prey.

8. *A Christmas Carol.*
9. Shirley Temple.
10. Oxford.

118

1. Larry Hagman.
2. False, he is a famous tennis commentator.
3. An ice skater.
4. A natural magnet.
5. Cairo.
6. Billie Holliday.
7. Aphids.
8. Charlotte Brontë.
9. He is a fashion designer.
10. The Peak District National Park.

119

1. *Bugsy Malone.*
2. True.
3. Worcestershire.
4. A substance that produces a chemical change without changing itself.
5. Belfast.
6. Heavy metal.
7. A squirrel.
8. Charles Kingsley.
9. Inspector Maigret.
10. A hobbit, in the book *The Hobbit* by J. R. R. Tolkien.

120

1. Clint Eastwood.
2. True.
3. Fifty.
4. The sewing machine.
5. Birmingham.
6. Police.
7. Bats.
8. They were all Poets Laureate.
9. The Prince and Princess of Wales.
10. A dance.

121

1. *Flashdance.*
2. False, it is 1 March.
3. Tennis.
4. Albert Einstein.
5. Turkey.
6. Status Quo.
7. A wild duck.
8. Mr Micawber, in Dickens's *David Copperfield.*
9. General Wolfe's.
10. Yorkshire.

122

1. Christopher Lee.
2. True.
3. A ball which pitches near the batsman and passes beneath his straight bat.
4. The vacuum flask.
5. Northamptonshire.
6. As Stevie Wonder.
7. Mouse and rat.
8. The theatre, he is a playwright.
9. His *Letter from America* radio broadcasts, which have been presented for many years.
10. Mount Rushmore.

123

1. Esther Rantzen, on *That's Life!*
2. True.
3. Yes.
4. Astronomy.
5. A group of Greek islands.
6. Jackie Wilson.
7. Over forty.
8. Puccini.
9. Nigel Lawson.
10. Four.

124

1. *Entertainment USA.*
2. False, it took place in 1926.
3. Manchester United.
4. A positively charged particle of matter.
5. Belgium.
6. U2.
7. Fish.
8. *Great Expectations.*
9. The Russian royal family.
10. Paddington Bear.

125

1. *Pinocchio.*
2. True.
3. Show jumping.
4. Yellow.
5. The Pyramids.
6. No, they made a record called 'I Wanna *Hold* Your Hand'.
7. Buried in the mud at the bottom of ponds.
8. He designed wood engravings.
9. He was an explorer who led the expedition which found the magnetic south pole.
10. A fish.

126

1. Cartoon characters – Heathcliff is a ginger cat and Marmaduke is a Great Dane.
2. False, it is the Severn Tunnel. The Totley Tunnel is the second largest.
3. He beat the reigning champion Boris Becker in the second round.
4. Force.
5. Berlin.
6. Buddy Holly.
7. A filly.
8. The cello.
9. A writer of crime novels.
10. Salisbury (123 metres/404 feet high).

127

1. Grace Kelly.
2. True.
3. Tennis.
4. It absorbs energy from the sun enabling plants to create food by photosynthesis.
5. Tunis.
6. Bob Dylan.
7. Long-haired cats.
8. Handel's *Messiah*.
9. Prime Minister of Eire.
10. The fifteenth.

128

1. Jack Lemmon, Tony Curtis and Marilyn Monroe.
2. False, it is Italian for 'Good evening'.
3. She was the youngest player ever to win Wimbledon (15 years and 285 days old).
4. Mathematics.
5. Beaulieu in Hampshire.
6. The Pet Shop Boys.
7. Potato.
8. Alfred, Lord Tennyson.
9. A Scottish outlaw (his real name was Robert Macgregor).
10. Britain will return it to the Chinese.

129

1. Ryan O'Neal and Tatum O'Neal.
2. True.
3. Racing – he's a jockey.
4. Gases.
5. They were both destroyed by an eruption of Vesuvius in AD 79.
6. 'Lucy in the Sky with Diamonds'.
7. No.
8. Verdi.
9. She was the first woman to fly solo from England to Australia (May 1930).
10. A French vegetarian dish of aubergines, courgettes, tomatoes, green peppers, onion, garlic and olive oil.

130

1. *Starsky and Hutch.*
2. False, he was a motor cycle racing champion and racing driver.
3. Show jumping.
4. Windsor.
5. It is on the opposite side of the River Tamar.
6. As Ringo Starr.
7. Monkeys have tails, apes do not.
8. John Keats. It is called 'To Autumn'.
9. He is the Prime Minister.
10. Jewellery and goldsmithing.

131

1. Neil.
2. False, he is an American film director.
3. Steffi Graf.
4. Eleven months.
5. Berne.
6. Bruce Willis.
7. By counting the rings on its scales.
8. Painting.
9. Samuel Crompton.
10. Sodium fluoride.

132

1. A Volkswagen car.
2. True.
3. Joe Louis.
4. A burette has a tap.
5. Amsterdam.
6. Nineteenth.
7. Whales, dolphins, dugongs and porpoises. (Any three from this list.)
8. *Timon of Athens.*
9. He was an artist.
10. Mrs Pepperpot.